THE SOUKOTTA STORY

Torn Curtain Publishing
Wellington, New Zealand
www.torncurtainpublishing.com

© Copyright 2022 Marissa Knott. All rights reserved.

ISBN Softcover 978-0-473-64025-5
ISBN Hardcover 978-0-473-64079-8
ISBN EPub 978-0-473-64026-2

No portion of this book may be reproduced, stored in a retrieval system or transmitted in any form or by any means—electronic, mechanical, photocopy, recording or otherwise—except for brief quotations in printed reviews or promotion, without prior written permission from the author.

Unless otherwise noted, all Scripture quotations are from the ESV® Bible (The Holy Bible, English Standard Version®), copyright © 2001 by Crossway, a publishing ministry of Good News Publishers. Used by permission. All rights reserved.

Scripture quotations marked NIV are taken from the Holy Bible, New International Version®, NIV®. Copyright © 1973, 1978, 1984, 2011 by Biblica, Inc.™ Used by permission of Zondervan. All rights reserved worldwide. www.zondervan.com.

Cataloguing in Publishing Data
Title: The Soukotta Story
Author: Marissa Knott
Subjects: Missions, Biography, Spiritual life, Indonesia.
Typeset in Minion Pro and Trade Gothic Next.

A copy of this title is held at the National Library of New Zealand.

Sam and Carol are two of World Outreach's most senior, experienced and esteemed missionaries. Their devotion to the Lord, his Cause and his Church is a living testament to the character of this godly and dedicated couple. I am constantly encouraged by their vision, passion, tireless energy and commitment to training and mobilising people for church planting and ministry. The influence of their lives across the Indonesian archipelago is incalculable. They are highly respected leaders, a true 'mother and father' in the faith, and an example to younger generations of leaders of how to serve God with all your heart. I'm delighted this book has been written about their lives and pray you'll be inspired by it.

—Bruce Hills
International Director, World Outreach

Pastors Samuel and Carolyn Soukotta have devoted their lives to the growth and development of the church and to Christian education in their beloved Indonesia. Their faithfulness to their vision, submission to the leading of the Holy Spirit and faith-filled life are an inspiration and blessing to many.

The success of their leadership is undergirded by a life of integrity. They are known and respected as a couple who bring passion, faith and optimism to every situation. From a young age, Rev. Samuel Soukotta understood his calling as an evangelist and apostolic leader in the Body of Christ. Since then, he and his wife have taken significant risks and sacrificed greatly to outwork the calling God has given them.

Today, God's work in Indonesia is thriving. In part, this is due to their years of endurance, godly character, and strong family life. Their story is one that will bring a fresh and biblical paradigm to Christian leadership. My prayer is that through these two servants of God, readers will be inspired and motivated to apply the principles they have lived by. I believe that as a result of this book, many quality leaders will be birthed and raised up to continue their legacy in Indonesia and around the world.

—Dr. Kalis Stevanus, MTh
Academic Dean, Sekolah Tinggi Teologi Tawangmangu
(Tawangmangu Bible College)

My first visit to Sam and Carol at Tawangmangu Bible College in Indonesia was in 1981. This trip challenged my thinking about missions and set me on a course of helping missionaries and those serving Christ off the shores of New Zealand.

I have always been impressed by Sam's strong convictions and his sense of humour, especially when he was interpreting. Carol has always carried the poise of a stateswoman and possesses a godly, no-nonsense commitment to her faith and the cause of Christ.

Together, over many decades, they have maintained their mission focus without deviation, being a couple showing persevering faith in action, and taking seriously their goal to prepare the younger generation to serve Christ. I honour them as a couple and commend them for the work they have achieved for Christ.

—Ps Kem Price
Director of Missions (1983-2003), New Zealand Assemblies of God

THE SOUKOTTA STORY

A LIFETIME OF FAITH IN INDONESIA

MARISSA KNOTT

My people, hear my teaching;
listen to the words of my mouth.
I will open my mouth with a parable;
I will utter hidden things, things from of old—
things we have heard and known,
things our ancestors have told us.
We will not hide them from their descendants;
we will tell the next generation
the praiseworthy deeds of the Lord,
his power, and the wonders he has done.
He decreed statutes for Jacob
and established the law in Israel,
which he commanded our ancestors
to teach their children,
so the next generation would know them,
even the children yet to be born,
and they in turn would tell their children.
Then they would put their trust in God
and would not forget his deeds
but would keep his commands.

Psalm 78:1-7 (NIV)

CONTENTS

Foreword — 1
Preface — 3
   Chapter One — 7
   Chapter Two — 15
   Chapter Three — 21
   Chapter Four — 27
   Chapter Five — 35
   Chapter Six — 41
   Chapter Seven — 47
   Chapter Eight — 55
   Chapter Nine — 61
   Chapter Ten — 65
   Chapter Eleven — 71
   Chapter Twelve — 77
   Chapter Thirteen — 83
   Chapter Fourteen — 89
   Chapter Fifteen — 93
   Chapter Sixteen — 99
   Chapter Seventeen — 103
   Chapter Eighteen — 113
   Chapter Nineteen — 121
   Chapter Twenty — 129
   Chapter Twenty-one — 137
   Chapter Twenty-two — 147
   Chapter Twenty-three — 155
   Chapter Twenty-four — 165
   Chapter Twenty-five — 173
   Chapter Twenty-six — 181
Afterword — 185
Acknowledgements — 195

FOREWORD

"You need to write your parents' story." It was more an impression than a direct word from God. Nevertheless, I knew the Lord was asking me to do this.

My response was that it was a great idea, but I thought the execution could be a bit challenging. After all, I live in New Zealand and they were in Indonesia—and although technology has come a long way, internet connection to the mountains in Java is still unreliable at the best of times.

I tucked the idea away in the back of my mind and decided it was something to pick up when circumstances were more ideal. That time came in March 2021 when Mum and Dad came for an extended break and stayed in our family home in Wellington, New Zealand.

Every day for several weeks we 'went to work', gathering at my family table, hot drinks on hand as they told their story whilst I typed as fast as I could, collecting as many details as possible. There were so many stories (too many to fit in this book), and it became a special time for me as I sat and listened for hours as they talked, laughed, reminisced, and most of all, recounted the goodness of God.

It was sweet. It was sacred. It was worship.

Writing Mum and Dad's story has been an incredible privilege and blessing for me. Not everyone has the opportunity to do what I have done, and I carry their story in my hands with the utmost respect and love.

I believe in a God of generations. In the Bible He is referred to as the God of Abraham, Isaac, and Jacob. This speaks of lineage—a family line where *His* story, passed on from one generation to the next, is lived out in daily expressions of faith. My parents' story is just this, a story of living faith that has shaped my life and will continue with my children and their children after them.

It is my prayer that through this book, many will be inspired to take God at His word and take steps of faith as my parents have done.

This is their story.

PREFACE

Smack!

The man's fist hit my jaw and sent me reeling. He was a seasoned man of the sea, sturdy, with arms well-developed from rowing and pulling nets laden with fish.

Whack!

I didn't have time to recover before the next hit came—this time to my side.

All traces of fear instantly disappeared as pain coursed through my body. I sprang to action, trying to defend my skinny frame but he was rapidly joined by the others, and before long I was knocked to the ground. One against many, I lay helpless on the floor as they converged on me, kicking and punching.

How had it come to this? Several days earlier, I had arrived on one of the Maluku islands of Indonesia after being invited by the Assemblies of God to speak in a series of meetings in their recently-planted church. People had come in droves to hear me, the young evangelist from Ambon, and so far, most had welcomed the messages.

Some, however, had not.

I had simply preached Christ, the One by whom we are saved. The church was packed and people spilled outside, sitting around the perimeter of the building and watching through the windows. I'd spoken about hell, and our need to come humbly to the feet of Jesus to ask for forgiveness. But my message was so different to what the local population was accustomed to hearing in the traditional church, and it grated on some—to the point that they became visibly incensed and angrily left the meeting.

As I lay there on the floor of the house next to the church where I had preached, my mind went back to earlier in the day when I had heard a commotion. A crowd had gathered outside the church and with angry voices began shouting, "Heretic, heretic. Let's kill the heretic."

Fear began to grip my mind as I realised that they were after *me*. They started throwing rocks at the church building, and with every crash, fear grew inside me. I had nowhere to go. The only exit was through a door in full view of the mob, so I waited, desperately hoping that someone would come to my aid.

It was only a matter of minutes before they realised there was no one inside the church building, and their focus turned to the house next door, where I was staying. Suddenly the door crashed open, and ten or eleven angry men burst in. I recognised them as the ones who had become angry at one of the meetings I'd spoken at. In fact, the leader appeared to be one of the elders of the nearby traditional church. Clearly, they viewed me as a heretic who needed to be silenced. They had found their target. Soon I was surrounded. Even if I wanted to, I could not move.

From the corner of my eye, I noticed some movement in the doorway and discovered that the older ladies who were hosting me in their home, had arrived. Hearing shouting, they had come to help. For a fleeting moment, my heart leapt. Help had come! This was short-lived, however, as they, too, were knocked to the ground. The sense of injustice grew within me—I could not believe my attackers would pick on women of their age.

Where were the police? I thought. That's when I realised that even the police were likely members of the traditional church and therefore reticent to come to my aid.

Kick after kick came and my body screamed as if it was on fire. As the assault went on, my mind kept churning until one crystal-clear thought emerged.

This is it. My time is up. Tonight, I will be in heaven.

In that moment, time seemed to stand still.

Eventually help did arrive—in the form of the army—and the group reluctantly dissipated. I was seriously bruised and pummelled, but still alive, and miraculously, there were no broken bones. I was thankful that the Lord had protected me from any long-term physical damage.

The senior army officer strongly advised me to leave the village until I could catch the next boat back to Ambon which was due in a couple of days. He would arrange an escort for my safety, but for the time being I needed to lay low.

For the next two days I hid in the forest while my hosts kept me fed and watered by secretly sending a runner with supplies. I was glad for the protection the forest provided, and for the time to think over and process what had transpired.

The boat ride back to Ambon was uneventful except for the stares of other passengers when they saw my face which had turned black and blue, and was distorted by swelling. I looked a sight! Now that the adrenalin from the last few days had worn off, not only was my body throbbing and achy, but my emotions were also on edge and I found myself jumping in panic at loud noises.

I was glad to reach the shores of Ambon, but apprehension started to nag as I approached my parents' home. My stepfather was the Police Commissioner for the district. *Had he heard what had happened? Did he know the police had not come to my rescue?* I stepped inside the house, and for a moment he quietly looked at my face, battered and bruised, then turning to my escorts he said, "My wife and I are so proud of our son. He didn't get beaten up for doing bad things. He was persecuted because he preached the Gospel."

To hear my stepfather's words and know that he was proud of me for spreading the good news of Christ was a balm to my soul. It had not always been this way with my family. . .

CHAPTER ONE

I was the second child of Ambonese parents who divorced early in my childhood. My mother, Jephsina, remarried, and in the process inherited two stepchildren. To ease tensions between our joint siblings, my sister and I spent more and more time living with our grandparents. As the years went on, my mother and stepfather had seven more children, and my grandparents' home became a refuge for me.

From early on, I suffered dreadful asthma. There was rarely a day that I did not have an attack and struggle to breathe. Unfortunately, asthma inhalers were not available then. As a result, my childhood was restricted as I was unable to play sport or games that involved running, in case of a flare-up. Some attacks caused me to panic. It often felt as if I was going to die.

My parents tried everything, and for years spent much time and money on remedies. I tolerated the daily spoonful of cod liver oil, and there were also regular steroid injections which helped for a short time but nothing more.

One day, after a particularly intense bout of asthma, my parents, in desperation, decided to take me to see a witch doctor. Although they attended the traditional church, they did not have a personal relationship with Christ, and as their church also practised spiritualist rituals, they saw no problem with this. In fact, the witch doctor herself was a member of the same church!

Dressed in black from head to toe with hair hanging limp to her waist, she waved her hands over me, chanting incantations as she swayed. We were hopeful for a cure, but her chants did not affect my sickness, and we returned home disappointed.

◆ ◆ ◆

Whether it was from work stresses, marriage and family issues, or both, my stepfather, Dan, eventually succumbed to heavy drinking. He would often come home from work reeking of alcohol. My stepfather was not usually an angry man, but when he drank his temper would escalate quickly. On those occasions, I would remain in my room, not wanting to rouse his emotions in any way. One night when I was about ten years old, he came home stone drunk. From my room, I could hear him stumbling about, muttering incoherently, and throwing his shoes around the house. By now I was accustomed to the highs and lows of his intoxication, so I waited for him to flop into unconsciousness, as was his standard practice.

Suddenly, the crack of a gunshot echoed through the house. The sound rang in my ears as it dawned on me that my stepfather had fired his gun at my mother! I wanted to run and hide, but I also wanted to check on Mum. But what might I find outside my room? I was fearful to open the door.

After what seemed like an eternity, my mother's door opened, and I heard her call my name. Relief washed over me in waves. The bullet had whizzed past her head, narrowly missing my mum's scalp but singeing her hair. She would not easily forget the smell of burning hair filling her nostrils.

◆ ◆ ◆

From this point, things did not get better, but neither did they get worse. My stepfather knew he needed help but instead tried to bury himself in his work as Police Commissioner for the district.

A couple of years later, as he was walking past the Assemblies of God church in downtown Ambon, my stepfather heard beautiful singing and felt drawn to go in. The Pentecostal movement was new to our region at the time, and the predominant feeling among the people was that they did not like it. They were content with the traditional church, which was historically Dutch Reformed; however, local beliefs and witchcraft had become part of their practice over the years, turning it into something it was never supposed to be.

With its emphasis on the Holy Spirit and salvation through Christ, the 'new' Pentecostal movement rattled religious and pious mindsets and was deemed heretical by the traditional church leaders. Many of them believed, and preached from their pulpits, that the Pentecostals were the end-time false prophets spoken of in the book of Revelation.

Favouring the pull of his heart over the voices in his head, my stepfather walked into the church that day and sat down at the back. When the preacher spoke, it was as if my stepfather was hearing the Word of God for the first time, and it ignited something in him. He felt as if the preacher was speaking exclusively to him, and at the invitation for people to accept Christ, ran to respond. At that altar, my stepfather, a hardened, angry man who was given to drink wept over all his sins and made peace with his Maker.

From that moment on, he joined the Pentecostal church where he had given his life to Christ, and stopped drinking and smoking, exchanging his addictions for a greater love. The man whom the community had long feared had now become someone who was given to tears every time he prayed.

My siblings and I all saw the difference and welcomed the transformation. Mum also noticed the change in her husband, but strangely, she did not like what she saw. She became agitated and unsettled, which puzzled my stepfather. She was not the vindictive type, but soon became resentful and critical. When my younger siblings cried, she began telling them they were cry-babies like their father, and whenever she saw him on his knees praying, she would walk around the house hitting pots and pans loudly to disrupt him.

My stepfather would try and tell her what he had experienced—that God's love was so real and that He loved her too, but she did not want to hear it. She had endured much conflict in the past, and her trust in him was broken. Adding to her strain was everything she had been taught in the traditional church which indicated that her husband was going down a wrong path. There was a battle going on in her mind, and an unseen battle for her spirit.

Soon after this, Mum became extremely sick, and the doctor said that she was to stay in bed because if she were to get up, she would not recover.

This news came as a shock to our whole family as she had always been a fit, healthy woman, not given to sickness. Standing beside her bed that night, I could see that she was in much pain, and my young mind was consumed with worry.

The day after the doctor's prognosis, however, my stepfather came home from work to find Mum out of bed, vastly improved! She described how, after he had gone to work that morning, she became aware of a presence in her room, and while lying in her bed suffering, a person's hand touched hers, and warmth radiated through her whole body. Mum did not recognise the person, but as she looked at the hand she noticed a wound in his palm, and instantly knew that it was Jesus. Now Mum was convinced of the reality of Jesus and His power, and my stepfather had the joy of leading her to Christ that very same day.

My mother was miraculously healed, and I watched her quickly progress from being weak and in pain to being able to get out of bed and walk around as usual. I had witnessed my first miracle of healing, and it left an indelible imprint on my mind.

◆ ◆ ◆

On the other hand, I still regularly battled asthma, and although I had witnessed a miracle of healing, there was no thought in my mind that perhaps the same power could heal me too. However, I was desperate to be well, and when my stepfather suggested I visit the church where he had found Christ and receive healing prayer, I agreed.

The sermon I heard that evening will remain in my memory my whole life. The pastor explained that Jesus was the answer to all our needs—healing included. At the end of his message, he invited people to raise their hands if they needed healing. Suddenly, my hand went up—without me moving it! In horror, I saw my younger brother Johnny sitting beside me, grinning from ear to ear. He was lifting my arm! Our father had instructed Johnny to ensure I responded to the healing call. At the appropriate time, he was to grab my hand and push it up in response.

A mixture of anger and embarrassment rose inside me. I was mad at my brother and felt humiliated in front of the congregation. I wanted to run to the back of the church and leave the building, but people had seen my hand, and I was too proud to back down now. Reluctantly, I inched my way to the front, but had no faith for a miracle, and when the pastor prayed for me, I did not feel anything change.

It wasn't until three days later that I realised something *had* happened. I could now breathe freely and easily. I had not had an asthma attack since the pastor prayed for me! Having suffered with asthma on an almost daily basis for my entire life, this was astonishing. There was no doubt about it—I, Sam Soukotta, long time asthmatic, had been miraculously healed! The excitement grew inside me, and I knew I had to tell my stepfather. He was the one who had encouraged me to go to the meeting, so he should know about my healing! I rushed to tell him what had happened, tripping over words as the story tumbled out of me. When I had finished speaking, my stepfather asked who had healed me.

At that moment, in a bolt of revelation, I knew that it was Jesus.

Jesus Christ had healed *me*—a young Ambonese boy. For the first time in my life, I was free from the curse of asthma. I was the grateful recipient of God's incredible healing power!

Now I was fully convinced that Jesus was real and that He was powerful. Not only had my mother been restored to perfect health, but I had too. Furthermore, my stepfather had been delivered from his addictions. I now knew that God was well able to heal *all* types of sickness and bondage.

I have never suffered another asthma attack since.

❖ ❖ ❖

Soon after my miraculous healing, my parents visited my grandparents' home, where I was staying. They clearly explained to me the good news that Jesus Christ came to give His life as a ransom for many, and that through Him, all humans can have a restored relationship with their Creator. That day, I asked Jesus into my heart. As I prayed the prayer of salvation, tears freely ran down my cheeks and I marvelled at the love of this Saviour who was so powerful and yet personal. That day my life changed. I was sixteen years old.

◆ ◆ ◆

Several months later while hanging out with friends at school, I was struck by the realisation that no one had ever told them about Jesus. I felt such a responsibility to share the Gospel with them but did not know how. I hated the thought that they might go to hell when they died, but my faith was still so new to me, and I felt like I did not have the right words.

I decided I needed to go to bible college to learn more about Jesus so I could more confidently speak about Him to others. After consulting with my pastor, I decided the Assemblies of God bible college would be the best choice.

My parents were incredibly supportive of this decision. They understood my yearning to know more about Jesus and His Word. Unfortunately, my extended family was adamantly opposed to this decision. Pentecostalism was a relatively new movement in Ambon, their churches tended to be small, and the pastors often didn't have a salary. They surmised that bible college would lead to a life of ministry, and consequently, they worried about my future and how I would make a living.

It all came to a head the night before my departure when my uncle, aunt and grandparents sat me down for a family meeting. At first it appeared they were genuinely concerned for my well-being, but as the night wore on and I stood my ground, they became more upset as they tried to dissuade me.

Not only were they concerned about my future prospects, they also expressed their opinion that I was joining a cult. In their mind, I would end up preaching heresy, and they would be humiliated by association. Emotions were running high, until one by one they began to curse me repeatedly.

"We would be happier if you were dead," one of them said.

"We curse you," said another.

"We ask the Lord to put sickness on you, that you would die. That would be better than bringing embarrassment to the family."

My uncle went so far as to take most of my clothes from my room and hide them, thinking this might deter me from going. They were convinced I was heading down the path of fallacy, and although they continued to admonish me through the night, my mind was made up.

Finally, as the long night gave way to the dawn, I gathered my few remaining belongings and prepared to leave. As I was about to leave, my uncle said, "Sam, when you walk out those doors, you are not part of this family anymore."

This was a defining moment for me. I loved my grandparents and uncle and aunt. They were more than just relatives—for many years they had looked after me as their son.

What my uncle said cut deep into my heart that day. I felt wholly rejected, but their words had not diminished my conviction. I knew without a doubt that God had called me into ministry, and more than anything in the world, I wanted to dedicate my life to serving Jesus. There were many unknowns ahead for me, but I believed my heavenly Father would look after me. Stepping out of the house, I set out on a journey of faith.

CHAPTER TWO

Bible college was a huge learning experience. I was now seventeen years old, and up to this point I had lived a comfortable and slightly pampered life, having had most things done for me. Now, I had to learn some life skills quickly. Even doing my own laundry was a new experience, but I soon became adept at washing and ironing clothes—not with a washing machine, but hand-washing, and using a heavy charcoal iron instead of an electric one.

For the first time in my life, I felt poor. Life at bible college was by no means luxurious—in fact, the students didn't even have what we would now consider essential. There were no beds or mattresses; instead, we all slept on thin mats. Food was simple, and unless a kind donor brought something special, dinner was usually rice, fish, and some greens. The dish I despised the most was the one we ate most frequently—leafy greens, picked from nearby bushes, boiled, and seasoned with salt. On several occasions when a police van arrived at the college, I would perk up knowing my stepfather had donated something for dinner.

Until bible college, I had never lacked anything. My stepfather was well remunerated for his work, and our family never wanted. In fact, we always had the best of whatever we needed. Now that my uncle had taken my clothes, I was left with three pairs of trousers and a few shirts. Had my stepfather known I was in need, he would have sent money, but I had decided it was time to start relying on the Lord's provision and not ask or hint to my parents that I required anything.

All bible college students had to do chores to help keep the college running, and one of the tasks we were assigned was to collect fresh water from the hill behind the campus. It was heavy work, and we had to walk through bushes with sharp, low-lying branches to get to the spring. After several weeks on this job, two pairs of my trousers were ripped entirely from the knees down and were unusable for anything but chores. That left me one good pair, but still, I did not want to ask my parents—I was waiting instead for my heavenly Father to provide. If His eye was on the sparrow, then He would also watch over me. That was His promise, and I was going to believe it!

On a holiday visit back home, I felt ashamed walking up the path to my parents' house. Being a perfectionist in nature, I had a high standard of dress and liked to maintain a tidy appearance. Wearing my only non-ripped trousers, which were starting to wear thin from overuse, my stepfather took one look at me and, after welcoming me, commented that I seemed to wear the same pair of trousers every time he saw me. I knew my stepfather didn't like to see his children dressing shabbily, but I had no other options, so I kept my mouth shut.

It was a thrilling answer to prayer when, not long into my stay, my stepfather offered to take me to the tailor[1] and have several new pairs of pants made for me. I was delighted that my heavenly Father would use my stepfather to provide my needs. This was a turning point in my reliance on God. From then on, I was confident the Lord would look after me—not simply to provide my needs, but to do so extravagantly and abundantly. I learned that day that when God gives, He gives more than enough!

Three years of bible college flew by, and although I was the youngest student in the college, I maintained good grades the whole way through. Coming top in my classes, I was given the platform to speak at my graduation, which was such an honour.

◆ ◆ ◆

After graduation, I set off with a friend on an itinerant speaking tour. We started with a couple of invitations, and I threw my heart into preaching. I loved speaking, and according to feedback, was a gifted speaker.

---

1 At the time, off-the-rack clothes were not available in Ambon

I was also discovering the other gifts God had placed on my life. One of these was the gift of healing.

Having personally experienced God's healing power as a teenager, I had no problem believing that Jesus could also heal others. I wanted to see people set free from suffering, and regularly looked for opportunities to pray for the sick.

My first healing miracle happened during a series of meetings in a small village church where I was the guest speaker. One night, a lady suffering from leprosy came forward for prayer after the message. The disease was eating her face, and the odour of decaying flesh was so powerful it was hard not to gag. Believing that God would heal her, I stepped out in faith, laid my hand on her head, and began to pray with fervour. Immediately the woman's skin started to change. Right before my eyes, the patchy skin, covered in lesions, became smooth and clear like a newborn baby! The transformation was extraordinary, and the woman was screaming and crying with joy as she touched her face. The atmosphere in the church was charged with excitement as people saw what God had done! All through the church, people were clapping and praising God, and a sense of anticipation filled the air. It was an incredible miracle, and I felt so excited that the Lord had moved in such a way.

The following night the same lady brought her father to the meeting. He was paralysed down one side, and depended on his walking stick to get around. I watched as this elderly man struggled to enter the church building, and anger started to build inside me at the sickness that had caused this man to be so restricted. I was angry at the devil who had come to *steal* this man's ability to walk, *kill* his joy of life and *destroy* his dignity. This was a holy anger!

After the service was over and the invitation was given, the man came forward for prayer. Expectation filled my heart. I had been waiting for this moment and believed that God wanted to heal him. With authority I declared over the man that he was not born to lean on a stick but to walk free. Then I commanded him to walk in Jesus' name. The man, who had seen the astounding transformation on his daughter's face, believed that

God could do the same for him. He started to straighten up. Like a creaky old door that gets a good oiling, his bones and muscles that had been dead were now responding to new life from the hand of his Creator. The walking stick was left on the church floor that night as God healed that man miraculously, and he walked out, free from his paralysis. Hallelujah!

Feeling humbled and grateful, I was thrilled that the Lord was so obviously working through me, and I knew my faith was growing through these experiences.

My younger brother Johnny was now also preaching, and we, along with three other young men from the Assemblies of God church, decided to team up to organise preaching rallies. We spent the next three years backed by the church, travelling all over the islands of Maluku, preaching the Word of God and leading many to Christ. It was during this time that we encountered unexpected resistance where I was beaten and called a heretic. However, we discovered that, even amidst the strong 'anti-Pentecostal' current, there was a deep hunger in people for the power and reality of God.

Those years were a rich time for all of us as we learned how to hear the Holy Spirit clearly and follow His leading, whether we were in small church gatherings or more significant rallies in town centres and football fields. It was valuable training ground as we developed in our giftings and proved our faithfulness with whatever God gave us to do.

After several years travelling around the Maluku Islands, we felt it was time to spread our wings and go further. We were beginning to receive invitations to speak in other parts of Indonesia and, as a team, were praying about where to go.

I had four invitations to go to Java, and was praying and fasting and asking the Lord which one to accept. After several days, I felt the Lord lay on my heart Surabaya, a large city in East Java, so I went to check my invitations, and one particularly caught my eye. It was from a group of travelling musical evangelists. The Asaph Band were booked to play at a number of open-air rallies, and they needed a speaker. It looked interesting to me, and on closer inspection I realised that Asaph had a month of upcoming rallies in the city of Surabaya! Buoyed on by this confirmation, I wrote to tell them I was coming.

♦ ♦ ♦

The three-day boat passage to Java sped by, and as my foot stepped on the dock in Surabaya, I felt like a new chapter in my life was about to open up and was eager to participate in all that God had in store for me.

The city was smelly and hugely crowded. I made my way as promptly as possible to the address where the Asaph band-members were staying. The lady of the house welcomed me in and told me to wait in the lounge while she went to let the team know I had arrived.

This was it! My new venture was about to begin. I waited patiently, briefcase in hand, ready to meet the team I would hopefully be working with for the next month, and who knew, maybe even longer!

A quiet "Selamat Pagi"[2] came from behind, and I turned to see a slender young woman coming towards me. The first thing that struck me was that although she spoke fluently, she was not Indonesian. With brown hair, green eyes and fair skin, she looked to be in her mid-twenties, but her calm manner made her seem more mature.

I said "Good morning" in response, and before I could even introduce myself, she asked me to follow her, then showed me to the room where all the gear was stored, whilst chatting about the sound system that had broken the night before. Thinking this to be a bit strange and wondering why she showed me the gear before introducing me to the rest of the team, I decided to be patient.

Europeans do things differently to us, I reasoned to myself.

She stood looking at me, waiting for an answer, and I realised I'd missed the question. "So can you?" she asked again, slightly impatient. "Can you fix it for the meeting tonight?" She pointed to one of the speaker units.

Ahh, so that was it! She was wondering if I could fix the sound system. Feeling a little confused, I told her, "I'm from Ambon. I just arrived today and came straight here like you asked."

---

2 Good morning

"Great," she responded offhandedly. "Do you think you'll get this done in time? Otherwise, we will have to work out something else for tonight."

She seems to speak the language fluently, I thought to myself, but she doesn't seem to understand quite as well.

"I've just arrived from Ambon," I reiterated, slower this time. "My name is Sam Soukotta. You invited me to come to Java—did you get my response?"

The moment I mentioned my name, recognition flickered, and she took a step back in surprise. She looked like she was seeing me for the first time.

"Sam Soukotta from Ambon? Oh, you're the preacher!" she replied, looking flustered. "I thought you were the technician coming to fix the sound system! We sent for you—I mean, *him*—this morning. I'm so sorry!"

She was embarrassed, but smiled as she extended her hand. "I'm Carol Walker, and I'm the one who sent you the invitation. Thank you for coming." We laughed together and I shook her outstretched hand, not realising I had just met my future wife.

CHAPTER THREE

Carol was the third child born to Dal and Dorothy Walker, church pastors in a small town in New Zealand. For several years they had felt stirrings in their hearts to go overseas as missionaries, and after much prayer and seeking wise counsel, they felt God directing them to Asia. So, in a step of obedience the young family packed their belongings, handed over the leadership of their church, and headed to Indonesia, eventually arriving on the island of Rote. It was 1949.

Moving from a quiet town in the South Island of New Zealand to a thatched-roof home in Indonesia's humid tropics was an extreme change for the Walker family. For Carol, at just four years of age, it was a jolt to her senses. Not only were they greeted by an abundance of flies, but the place was stiflingly hot. To make matters worse, their new home was situated directly behind an abattoir, and the smell of rotting blood was nauseating. If Carol's mum, Dorothy, had harboured any glamourous ideas of missionary life, these were quickly suppressed by their new surroundings.

The first year in Indonesia came with plenty of challenges for Carol's family. As well as learning a new language and adapting to a foreign culture, her parents had to find creative ways to make ends meet. Unfortunately, the financial support they had been promised took many months to arrive, and with no other source of reliable income, it was a tough way to start their new life. Vegetables were scarce on the remote island, and Dal and Dorothy struggled to get enough food for their family, often driving considerable distances to buy fresh food.

When both Dal and Dorothy fell sick with malaria, they decided they needed to find a better environment for the family, and before the year was up, the Walkers moved to the island of Java. This proved to be much more suitable for the family, and with a bigger, cleaner home and a more abundant food supply, they were happy to settle down in the city of Malang. Dal started teaching bible classes from their home and soon a bunch of keen young men were coming regularly to learn.

Dal loved getting amongst the local people to practise speaking Bahasa Indonesia, and quickly became fluent in the language. Dorothy also was able to make significant progress by speaking with the other mothers in the area as she kept an eye on her brood of young children plus a new-born baby.

On the day that Carol turned five years old, she happily hurried along the road to the local Dutch school, excited to start her new educational adventure and meet new friends. The Walker children had already started picking up the Indonesian language, but now they had to readjust to yet another foreign tongue under the tutelage of Dutch-speaking teachers. Adapting came with its own set of challenges. One day Carol and her siblings turned up to school only to find they were the only ones there! Not understanding the language, the Walker kids had missed the communication that it was a public holiday.

The following decade brought much change to Indonesia, particularly in the government. Under Dutch colonial rule, Indonesia's seventeen thousand islands had been divided into different states. Now, there was no strong government in place. This led to instability and chaos as various factions vied for the helm of a nation unused to governing itself. The political unrest of the 1950's meant that Carol and her family had to flee Indonesia several times for their safety.

If Dal and Dorothy had known what they were going to face when they first arrived in Indonesia, I wonder if they might have waited until the roller coaster was over before leaving their quiet home in New Zealand. In any case, they spent the greatest part of the next decade moving between New Zealand, the United States and Canada, waiting until it was safe for them to return. By now there were eight children in the family, but for Dal, who loved adventure and travel, the growing responsibility and constant uncertainty did not dampen his enthusiasm in the least. It was a trait he passed on to Carol from a very young age—the ability to keep a positive outlook in the face of challenging situations.

In her early teen years, Carol moved back to New Zealand to complete her high school education. Having always loved music but never able to pursue it, she had learned to play some tunes by ear, but now had the opportunity to take piano lessons. These classes strengthened her skill, and even though Carol only had a year's worth of formal training, it turned out to be a worthwhile investment. She practised every day, and was encouraged to play in church services, which she did on several occasions. Carol also had a lovely voice and enjoyed singing in the church choir. After graduating at the top of her class, she went on to do a secretarial course. Again, she excelled. Organisation and administration came naturally to her, and she was delighted to be doing something that she loved.

When Carol finished her studies, she returned to Indonesia to join her family. At this point, her two older brothers were still studying overseas, but Carol's parents and five other siblings were living in Bali—long before it was a famous tourist spot. One day not long after she arrived, Carol was walking along Kuta beach when she noticed a massive structure being built. Curious, she inquired of the builders, who told her they were constructing the first beachfront hotel in Bali. At that point, Carol could not see why people would want to holiday in such a simple and undeveloped spot, devoid of any luxury!

◆ ◆ ◆

In the three years that Carol had been away, her parents had founded a bible college and an orphanage that now housed ten children. Fitting right back in, Carol began helping her parents with communication, writing newsletters to their supporters and mission organisation. She was efficient at her work and loved feeling that she was part of a team and that her work was meaningful. In turn, Dal and Dorothy were finding satisfaction in their work as they invested in the community and people around them.

Unfortunately, this was not to last. Further political changes led to a resurgence of unease throughout the country and quickly things began to change. Carol first noticed this when the cost of essentials increased dramatically on a weekly basis. Basic commodities were becoming so expensive that it was sending many Indonesians to poverty. Wanting to do something about the impending crisis, passionate university students were gathering in the streets, encouraging the masses to raise their voices to protest the soaring costs of living.

Carol watched as the army presence in Bali went from being virtually non-existent to visibly prominent. Many of the soldiers looked like they had just come out of school, and she realised they were probably about the same age as her. They appeared so severe and uptight in their uniforms, but she wondered if they felt nervous and edgy like she did. When she walked home from the shops, easy-going locals who used to wave and smile from their homes now hid behind closed doors, fearful and timid. Army jeeps with well-armed corporals were now regularly patrolling the island, bringing tension to the local villagers and transforming the atmosphere of the island from laid-back and happy to one of unease.

One night while driving home from a meeting, the Walkers were stopped by an army patrol who instructed them to get out of the car and run and hide in the gutters beside the road. The officers told them this was a practise drill for what was coming—even though they wouldn't give any specifics on what that meant.

The family heard rumours that the Indonesian Communist Party were rousing, but these were never formally acknowledged in the media. Eventually, even listening to the news on the radio was banned, which Carol found frustrating as she wanted to know what was going on. Dal tried to quietly tune in to the BBC or any overseas stations but could not find conclusive news.

One day at the end of 1964, an official from the New Zealand consulate arrived on the Walkers' doorstep. Looking around furtively before he stepped into the house, he told them in hushed tones that they needed to leave the country immediately. He had travelled from Jakarta to Bali to warn all expats to leave. The New Zealand embassy staff could not even make phone calls anymore, for fear someone had bugged the phones.

Carol had an ominous sense that something terrible was coming. She could see the tension on her parents' faces as they prepared to pack up their belongings yet again. They were reticent to leave, and their hearts were torn as they hugged and kissed the orphan children, assuring them they would soon return. With a competent team of local staff, Dal and Dorothy were confident things would run well in their absence. Still, it was emotionally taxing to take their leave, especially as they had no idea why they were leaving or how long they would be away.

Carol, too, was sad to leave. Indonesia had a huge place in her heart, and despite having spent as many years living in other countries as she had in Indonesia, it was the place her family kept coming back to, and for her, it was now home.

The Walkers flew back to New Zealand, and over the next few months stayed glued to the radio and scanned the papers to glean any information they could on what was happening in Indonesia.

It all came to a head one night in late September 1965 when six of Indonesia's top military generals were kidnapped and then executed by the Indonesian Communist Party. This set in motion a political purge that led to mass killings which became known as the Indonesian genocide. It was a time of great stress and fear for those in Indonesia, and for the Walkers who were thousands of miles away, the news was shocking. Carol and her family tried to listen for every snippet of information they could and, saddened by what they heard, kept praying that the bible college students and orphans would be protected.

One day Dal and Dorothy received news that the bible college in Bali had closed its doors, and that one of the village pastors, an innocent bystander, had been shot and killed by mistake. It was senseless and numbing news, and Carol watched as her parents grieved his passing and grappled with not knowing what was happening at the orphanage. As far as they knew, the children were safe, but communications between New Zealand and

Bali were unreliable at best. It was a dark time for Dal and Dorothy and they could only hope.

As the months passed, Carol knew she needed to carry on with her life but wondered what her next step was. She had been waiting, along with her parents, for the situation in Indonesia to calm down, but with mass killings still happening and the country highly volatile, there was no way the Walkers would be returning to Indonesia anytime soon.

CHAPTER FOUR

While waiting to return to Indonesia, the Walkers had an opportunity to minister in the Philippines. Knowing they couldn't just sit in New Zealand doing nothing, Dal moved his family there and became immediately involved in running open-air campaigns. At this time World Outreach were looking for someone to help with administration in the Manila office, and having received correspondence from Carol when she was assisting her parents in Bali, they knew she was up to the task.

Thrilled at the proposal, Carol jumped at the opportunity. She knew that when God closes one door, He opens another, and this was what she had been waiting for! It was as if the Lord had tailor-made the role for her. By working with World Outreach, Carol could use her gift in administration while helping an overseas mission agency. It was everything she loved in a package.

Carol threw herself entirely into her new surroundings. The sights, smells, and sounds of Manila and the warmth of the locals enveloped her as she adapted to the new culture and language. Being musical, Carol was delighted to find the love for music so strong amongst the Filipino people.

Living in a new country filled Carol with excitement. She loved working and evangelising with the resident team and soon found herself overseeing the Manila office which also doubled as a distribution centre for Gospel literature. As part of her job, Carol and a couple of girlfriends were involved in city-wide evangelism. The trio would grab every opportunity to share the good news about Jesus, even when on public transport. Recognising that the passengers were a captive audience, the ladies would ask the bus driver to please turn down the music as they had an important announcement to make. One of the group would then proceed to preach a short message while the others gave out literature. They were always well received. Often, when they stopped at a red light, if another bus pulled up alongside them, the people in the bus beside them would also put out their hands to receive the leaflets—they did not want to miss out!

During this time, Carol discovered that a couple of the men she worked with at the office were part of a well-known Gospel singing quartet in the city. They decided to combine their evangelistic efforts, and from that point on they worked together, setting up in the outdoor 'plazas', where the quartet would sing—their fame making it easy to draw crowds. A simple Gospel message would then be preached and literature given to all who came.

They were vibrant times, and between her outreach with the quartet and her work with the mission agency, Carol found her time in the Philippines very rewarding. The government was particularly honouring of women, and Carol and her two friends found that when they asked for permission for evangelistic initiatives, this was easily granted. This favour led to them being able to go into the main men's prison. Every Saturday for over a year, the group of ladies had the opportunity to share the love of Jesus with the men on death row. It was a privilege to lead many of these men to Jesus in the last days of their lives.

In three years, Carol had grown so much in her reliance on the Lord and in hearing His voice, so it was a surprise when she began to feel that her season in Manila was coming to a close.

She loved the work and the people, but it all made sense when she spoke with her parents and heard that back in Indonesia, they needed practical help with a new bible college they had founded. As it turned out, her work in managing the Manila office and in founding the music team was excellent preparation for what God had in her future.

◆ ◆ ◆

As soon as the situation in Indonesia had settled down, Dal and Dorothy Walker returned to Indonesia. With very little to return to in Bali, they decided to move the family to Tawangmangu[3], a small town in Central Java surrounded by terraced rice paddies and bountiful vegetable gardens. Supported by some of the staff from their previous season in Bali, Dal and Dorothy wasted no time in establishing a bible college there. High in the mountains, it was also an area of respite and relaxation for local tourists wanting to escape the oppressive heat of the cities.

With the help of some friends, the Walkers bought a one-hectare site complete with a couple of buildings, and were working hard to build the profile of the bible college. Their work was paying off and within the first year, they had fifty enrolments and were attracting students from all over Java and some of the outer islands. The college was growing faster than they could keep up with but with only a handful of staff, the administration side of things soon got out of hand. There were papers and enrolment forms to process, bills to be paid, and invoices to be filed. They needed extra hands, and they knew Carol was the right person for the job.

Carol was excited at the prospect of serving with her parents again. Before her lay the opportunity to do something she loved, plus her parents were keen for her to establish a worship team similar to the one she had been working with in Manila.

◆ ◆ ◆

Carol had not long resettled in Indonesia when she formed the Asaph team—a musical band comprised of students and staff from the bible college. Between them there was a drummer, a bass player, a couple of guitarists, three singers, and Carol on the keyboards. It was a bigger group than the one in Manila, but Carol had a vision to do significant events and knew a good-sized team was needed.

The Asaph Band would work with local churches throughout Indonesia to set up open-air events in town centres and soccer fields. The churches would be responsible for the promotion and venue; the band would play, then an invited speaker would share the good news about Jesus. Carol was

---

3 Pronounced: Ta-wang-mang-u

in charge of setting up the calendar for the team and the practical logistics, including booking the speakers for each night's rally.

After the horrors of the past few years, many Indonesians were now searching for truth and hope. As churches saw many non-members walking into their services to surrender their lives to Jesus, pastors were recognising that the nation was wide open for the Gospel. It was the ripe time for a ministry like the Asaph Band, and opportunities were plentiful as churches seized the moment to host rallies. Although she was busier than she had ever been, Carol knew this was what God had gifted her for, and she felt comfortable in it.

Six months in, and the team was in full swing. So many people were attending the night rallies, and sensing there was growing hunger, the band added additional meetings as they went. Often, they would run five, seven or even ten nights in a row, the crowds building night upon night. They were hungry for an encounter with God, and He responded by blessing them with His presence. Some nights it was almost like they could reach out and touch heaven and Carol felt so privileged to be part of these sacred moments.

She was in her element. She loved organising the rallies, and playing the keyboard on stage, but most of all, she loved seeing people meet Jesus for the first time, their faces lighting up and hope filling their eyes.

◆ ◆ ◆

Carol writes:

I loved working with the band, but the one demand that seemed unrelenting was the pressure to find speakers for the rallies. Even though we were blessed to have a couple of outstanding preachers working with us on a rotating roster, they could only commit to several nights at a time due to family or other ministry commitments.

These men were gifted evangelists who could clearly communicate the good news to a non-Christian crowd and with great results. The evening rallies would build night upon night, and it seemed that the momentum could continue if only we had the opportunity to run four, five or even more consecutive nights. As a team we never wanted to restrict what the Lord was doing, but if the evening rallies were to continue for longer periods of time we would have to work quickly to find more preachers.

After several months of trying to do this, we decided it was time to introduce a full-time speaker as part of our team.

I immediately started an intensive search for the right person. We were familiar with many of the dynamic speakers on Java but decided to cast our net a bit wider, hoping to find just the right person—someone who wasn't already working for a local church and could be flexible with their time. We heard about a team of young speakers from Ambon, one in particular, by the name of Samuel Soukotta, who had a growing reputation in the islands as a powerful evangelist with a gift of healing. After hearing the name Samuel Soukotta a few times from various sources, I decided to send him an invitation to come and speak for us in Surabaya, where we had a month of rallies booked. I felt nervous about asking someone to preach that we had never met, and I was praying this Ambonese evangelist was all he was rumoured to be.

I felt the weight of responsibility for our team and, in a broader sense, for the rallies, but we committed it to the Lord, and I put it aside to focus on the task at hand. We had our own musical preparation to do for the upcoming rallies and not a lot of time to rehearse.

A few weeks later, we were in Surabaya. Our rallies were to be held in a field located at a busy intersection of roads, with many people coming and going. We set up a stage and had stacked sound systems on top of each other to carry the sound of the music and preaching over the hubbub of the daily busyness. The first night had gone well until the end of the meeting when one of the sound system speakers had blown. Our bass player promptly booked a technician to come and fix it, knowing that we would need it the next night.

On the morning of our second day in Surabaya, I was relaxing in my room upstairs in our host's expansive house when there was a knock on the door. I opened it to the lady of the house, who informed me that there was a man here for the Asaph team, and could I please come and speak with him?

Oh good, that will be the technician, I thought.

Wondering why our host didn't ask one of the men in our band to attend to him, I followed her downstairs.

The man was standing, waiting in the foyer, briefcase in hand.

He probably has more equipment outside in his car, I presumed.

I noticed the man in front of me was handsome and very slim, with a strong jawline and curly dark hair, and for a technician, he was immaculately dressed. I didn't catch his name but caught the end of his introduction that he was Ambonese.

Motioning for him to follow me to the gear room, I explained how the speaker had blown at the end of last night's meeting and how we really needed it fixed quickly.

He was quiet and didn't seem to be very interested in the sound system. I hoped he knew what he was doing.

"Can you fix it for the meeting tonight?" I asked.

He looked confused and repeated that he was from Ambon and had come as quickly as he could.

Good for you, I thought, but out loud I said, "Do you think you can have this speaker fixed so that we can use it tonight, please?"

The man was quiet, and the silence was becoming a bit awkward.

Why doesn't he answer me?

Not knowing quite how to handle the situation, I was beginning to lose patience with our technician who didn't seem to want to do his job.

Finally, he spoke again, this time a little slower. "I've just arrived from Ambon. My name is Sam Soukotta. You invited me to come to Java. Did you get my response?"

Goodness, there he goes again, with his ethnicity! I thought.

But wait . . . Sam Soukotta? Why does that name sound familiar?

Right at the back of my mind, recognition was slowly growing. I realised that his name was familiar to me because I had personally written to him. My face began to heat up with embarrassment.

Oh no! In a case of mistaken identity, I had thought this man was coming to fix our speaker when in fact, he *was* the speaker! The next few minutes were spent in humble apologies as he graciously laughed it off. We shook hands and I decided to start again.

"I'm Carol Walker, and I'm the one who sent you the invitation. Thank you for coming."

CHAPTER FIVE

By the time I joined Asaph they were a well-established band providing excellent praise and worship for evangelistic rallies all around Java. Coming onto the team at this point was a privilege.

The spiritual atmosphere in Java was very different to what I was used to in Ambon. Islam was still the main religion, but there were also many flourishing, Spirit-filled churches that functioned separately from the traditional church. I found this very interesting. In Ambon the churches were predominantly traditional, often with paganism mixed in. This created a culture which was not open to the Holy Spirit, although this had been gradually changing over the last few years.

In Java, however, the churches were vibrant and eager to partner with the Asaph team to run evangelistic rallies.

This was my first time working with a band, and it was a good fit. As the speaker, linking up with a great band of musicians allowed for a level of momentum and reach that I hadn't had before. Together we realised that the combination of excellent, passionate worship and fired-up, anointed preaching was impactful. I was also grateful to have ministry friends. When they invited me to join their team long-term, I gladly accepted. It was a win-win situation for all of us.

Having a base at the Tawangmangu Bible College brought a sense of stability and belonging when we weren't travelling. Our tours were scheduled in advance so that we could stay in one location for up to five days. If the crowds were growing, we often stayed longer. It was tiring but rewarding work.

It didn't take long for me to get into the rhythm of packing down at the end of each meeting, transporting the instruments and sound gear back to our accommodation and then setting it all up again the next day.

As a Christian band travelling in a Muslim country we were bound to run into opposition, and it happened soon enough in one of the rallies near the Surabaya airport.

The meeting started as usual, with the band leading praise and worship. The field was located in a bustling part of the city, near a main road. That night, many onlookers stopped, attracted by the crowd and the music. I could feel momentum gathering. As the worship leaders encouraged us to look to Jesus in our singing, hands were going up in worship. The bystanders were engrossed.

One of the ladies from the local church who was working with us noticed a man standing near the side of the stage in a restricted area. He seemed to be fiddling with the cables that were powering our equipment. That's when she noticed he had wire cutters in his hand, and realised he was trying to cut the cables! Quickly she moved towards him, motioning some of her teammates to follow. As she neared the scene, she could see he seemed agitated and was no longer interested in the cables but was frantically massaging his wire-cutting arm. Much to the lady's surprise, she realised that his arm had frozen in position as he reached to cut the wires. He was now stuck with his hand fixed in the air! He couldn't seem to relax his arm or bring it down. When the lady from the church offered to have someone pray for him because Jesus could heal him, the man ran off down the road in a panic, his arm still up in the air. Whatever mischief he had planned, amounted to nothing.

Meanwhile, as Carol was playing the keyboard and looking out over the crowd, she noticed a young boy not too far from the front. He was about sixteen years old, and unlike the other teenagers who were absorbed in the experience, this boy looked glum and seemed detached from what was happening around him. He had been like this most of the night, but as the meeting proceeded, Carol watched as the expression on his face changed from disinterest to shock and then to growing excitement until he was grinning from ear to ear.

He began to shout almost hysterically, "I'm healed! I'm healed," at which point I went over to him to find out what he had been healed from. I discovered that the young man had been born deaf and for sixteen years had not been able to hear or speak. During the praise and worship, the Lord had beautifully and instantly healed him—without anyone even praying for him! For the first time in his life, he was able to hear and speak clearly. The mayor of the village happened to be standing beside the boy. He too was amazed. He knew the young man personally and confirmed that an undeniable miracle had taken place.

My mind began processing what had happened. Up until this point I had only ever experienced healings when praying for people—commonly with my hand on or near their point of pain.

This was different. It was still a sovereign move of God, but there was a new dimension that I had not known before. A sense of awe at the greatness of God settled on me as I understood that He did not need my human involvement to work and yet He still *chose* to work through me. The revelation both surprised and thrilled me.

That night as we worshipped, my Lord had come. In the words of scripture, He was enthroned by our praises. Jesus had walked around the room that night and touched this young man! My expectation was stretched, and my faith increased. No longer could I limit God to what I knew or had experienced in the past.

Several nights later, I had finished preaching and had just started to pray for the sick when there was a sudden commotion near the back of the crowd. I couldn't see what was happening, but as Carol was onstage playing the keyboard, she saw a man yelling excitedly as he made his way through the crowd. The people parted to allow him through, and he finally made it to the front. Banging his fists on the platform, he too shouted, "I'm healed! I'm healed!" I urged him to come up onto the platform with me to tell us what had happened, but before he even had the chance to speak, the crowd recognised him and went wild, clapping and cheering! This man was well known in his community. Twelve years earlier he had suffered a debilitating stroke, leaving him paralysed down one side. Unable to move freely, he had to drag his paralysed side as he walked, which was restrictive and painful. As he walked across the stage towards the microphone, the crowd erupted in joy and excitement! Everyone could see this man was walking normally again! God had touched him that night on the soccer field, and his miracle of healing was witnessed by all. Many salvations took place after that, as people surrendered their lives to a God whose power was evident among us.

Another night, on another field, I noticed a man leaning on crutches through the whole service. I found this both encouraging and challenging. As these were outdoor rallies, we did not supply chairs, and people often stood on the grass for two or more hours. This was a long time for someone in his condition. Was he seeking a miracle? *He must have some degree of spiritual hunger,* I thought. I carried on with my message, but my eyes kept being drawn to him and I sensed God wanted to heal him.

At the end of my message, I stepped off the stage and went directly over to the man. "Do you want to be healed?" I asked with a sense of expectation. "Yes, I do," he responded, nodding emphatically. I asked him to hand me his crutches which he gave to me unreservedly, even though he was unstable on his feet. It was wonderful to see him reaching out for a miracle in faith. Excitedly I declared, "In the name of Jesus, I command you to walk!"

Without any hesitation, the man placed one foot in front of the other, and began to walk perfectly. There was not even a wobble or a limp—his back was straight, and his steps confident! The people around who watched the miracle happen clapped and hollered. The man was beside himself with joy as he walked away from that meeting, free from his crutches. Praise the Lord! It was such a beautiful miracle. What an amazing God we serve!

The faith of our band was activated as we witnessed God's supernatural power, and although the work was demanding and often required long hours, we felt energised and fresh after every service. By now we had begun to expect God to move miraculously whenever we ministered. However, for many people who came to our rallies, seeing miracles was still a phenomenon.

During the month in Surabaya, our team stayed in the home of a woman who had never witnessed a miracle before. She had attended the rally the night the man with crutches was healed and had seen God work supernaturally with her very eyes, but she still didn't know what to make of it. That night, she tossed and turned in her bed, unable to sleep. She was sceptical. How could a man who was so obviously dependent on his crutches walk away perfectly healed? How did a miracle like that happen? She wanted to believe this was genuine, but her logic told her it was impossible.

The following day she rose early and made her way to the area where the meeting was held the night before, hoping to find the man who had been healed. If she could talk to him, she might get some answers, she thought.

As she neared the area, she saw people had gathered, and got out of the car to see what was happening. Maybe someone could point her in the direction of the man she was looking for? Walking over to the group, she was amazed to find they were all looking in wonder at the man who was healed the night before! There he was, walking around, enjoying his legs, and telling all who would hear that Jesus had healed him.

Her heart pounded as she watched and listened. Genuinely absorbed in what she was witnessing, and desperate for proof, she went over to talk to the man, pressing him for the full details of what had happened the previous night.

When she walked away from that conversation, the war between her head and her heart was settled. Jesus wasn't just a character from the bible or a famous person from history—He was real! Now she believed, deep down, that Jesus was near to her and that His power is still at work in the world. From that day on, the woman attended every meeting we held in her city. She was so hungry to see God's power and reality that she did not want to miss anything.

And she was not the only one. As the Lord performed miracles, the crowds kept growing night after night as non-believers were attracted to what was happening. They knew people in the meetings who had suffered, often for years, and they wanted to see God heal them.

Having also struggled with extreme asthma, I understood what it was like to have a debilitating sickness. I had experienced God's healing power in my life as a teenager and knew that these miracles were one way for people to see God's reality and power. Indeed, many who came to witness the healing of others also experienced salvation for themselves. I was in awe that the God of the whole universe, the Creator of heaven and earth, would work through me in the area of supernatural healing! It was the same amongst our team. We knew that we were part of something incredibly significant and felt privileged that God was doing wonders among us.

CHAPTER SIX

In some ways, I was becoming well known around the country as a preacher and healing evangelist, but it was Carol who held the team together and kept us on track. She handled the logistics of the team's movements efficiently and calmly, and her interactions with the pastors and churches we worked with were always gracious and accommodating. She threw herself wholeheartedly into each venture, but when the unexpected happened, as it sometimes did, she was calm, wise, and decisive.

I realised that the degree of impact we were having was in no small part due to her ability to organise so well, and I respected her for it. Apart from being obviously gifted in many areas including music, administration, and leadership, Carol was also amiable and approachable. The fact that she looked different from any Indonesian, didn't seem to register with her—she thought of herself as one of us.

Over time, our relationship grew from respectful working mates to good friends. Carol admired my single-minded devotion to Christ. She told me she had never met a young man who was so passionate about Jesus, and she encouraged me in this. Our friendship was easy and uncomplicated as we shared the same passion for serving Jesus and seeing as many people come to know Him as possible.

One day about six weeks into our tour, in a time of team prayer, Carol was fervently praying out loud for God's blessing on the meeting that night. I was silently joining in agreement when, out of the blue, I felt the Lord impress on me that Carol was to be my wife! This came as such a surprise to me. Although I thought she was a lovely lady, our friendship was so recent, and there were no romantic feelings. *That's a bit sudden, Lord,* I thought. But knowing better than to doubt what I felt was a prompt from

God, I kept it quiet and wrote the impression as an entry in my journal.

Strangely enough, as the weeks passed, feelings for Carol begin to grow in my heart, and every now and then when I caught her looking at me, it seemed that she was feeling the same way towards me. Knowing that who we marry is one of the biggest decisions a person can make in life, I spent much time praying into this. I felt clearly that the Lord had spoken to me about marrying Carol, but I wanted to be absolutely sure that my timing was right, and not rushed. Also, at this point I really wasn't sure how she felt.

One day when we were together, I decided it was time to test the waters to see where she stood. Not knowing how to broach the subject, and feeling so nervous I was tongue-tied, I resolved instead to let my journal do the talking. Shoving my diary under her nose, I pointed to the entry which read: *Carol Walker is going to be my wife.* It was a rather forward way of telling someone you liked them, but I had no intention of dating for the sake of dating. This was not a whim, and I didn't want to waste her time or hurt her.

My heart pounded as I waited for her response. Thankfully, Carol was not overly emotional. On reading the note, she simply said, "I'm not surprised," smiled at me, and handed me back the journal. In her pragmatic way, Carol was saying yes, and as we compared notes, I was overjoyed to discover that she loved me too and believed God had brought us together.

In my culture, when one intends to marry his beloved, a representative from the man's family goes to the girl's family to ask the parents for her hand in marriage. I didn't have any family close by, and thought about who from my family could represent me. Meanwhile, I decided to speak to Carol's father, Dal.

I knew the Walker family well, but still there were nervous butterflies in my stomach as we told Carol's parents that we had started dating. However, I needn't have worried. Dal and Dorothy were so happy to hear the news and immediately assumed that we would be married before long! I walked out of our short meeting having received Dal's blessing and Carol's hand in marriage—no representative needed! *That was easy,* I thought. *I like the way these people do things!*

Just four months later, on Carol's twenty-seventh birthday, we were married. If someone had told me on leaving Ambon that I would be married in a little over a year, I would not have believed them, but here we were, husband and wife, and how exquisite she looked!

◆ ◆ ◆

Our ministry dates had been booked long before our wedding, and squeezing in a honeymoon proved challenging. Our team was due to go to Ambon for meetings the following week, so we decided that Carol and I would leave a few days earlier. I wanted to show my new bride my hometown and introduce her to family and friends who had not been able to attend our wedding.

This plan suited us perfectly. For many years Carol had heard about the famed beaches of Ambon and had experienced the beautiful voices and musical talents of the Ambonese students who attended the bible college. She was excited to see where I grew up. With a romantic picture of the two of us walking hand-in-hand on white sandy beaches and beautiful music wafting in the background, we had high expectations of our honeymoon. This was going to be our first holiday together!

On our first night in Ambon, my parents hosted a dinner at our home. This turned out to be no small affair! My parents were so proud to introduce their daughter-in-law to everyone. Aunts, uncles, grandparents, cousins and even distant relatives crammed into the lounge, sitting on benches along the walls. Everywhere we looked there were children, all wanting to meet my new bride. Although Carol was able to converse fluently in the Indonesian language, she had not come across the Ambonese dialect before and struggled to understand what people were saying, so I became her translator for most of the night—and for the rest of our time in Ambon. The gathering continued into the late hours, with Carol the centre of attraction.

From that night on, we were never left alone. Carol was like a magnet, especially for the children, who were intrigued by the 'lady with white skin' who was now one of them.

We did get to walk the sandy white beaches hand-in-hand. However, perhaps to Carol's disappointment, we were by no means alone, and there were no melodic sounds in the background.

Soon the remaining Asaph team arrived and we started holding meetings in some of the villages. These were mostly small gatherings held on the front lawns of family and friends' homes. In my heart was a burning passion to tell my people how much Jesus loved them and that He had died for them. Having grown up in the culture and been a part of the traditional church, I knew how much they were missing without a personal relationship with Jesus.

The spiritual atmosphere over the Maluku Islands was dark at the time, and there were very few bible-based, Spirit-filled churches. Instead of being a beacon of light and hope to their communities, the traditional church had mixed religious traditions with animism and the occult. In doing this, they had diluted the power of the Gospel and unwittingly given the devil a foothold, to the point where those who attended church lived no differently from the rest of the population. It was no wonder that some in the community were angered when our team worshipped, preached with power, and prayed for miraculous healing.

On a couple of occasions, while we were worshipping on our friends' front yards, groups of young people threw large stones at us. During one of these incursions, I watched as the stones fell short of me, but unfortunately Carol was hit on the head while playing the keyboard. She was okay at the time, and to her credit she chose to ignore it. Continuing to play, she prayed the Lord would protect the team and change the hearts of the young offenders.

We knew the people weren't bad, but we also understood that in the spiritual realm we were contending with demonic forces who were in opposition to the Holy Spirit. Praise and worship always provokes the Enemy. When we invite the Holy Spirit and worship Jesus, we enthrone Him in that place—and when Jesus' presence comes, the devil runs away!

Soon after this, our honeymoon became even more memorable when my wife tripped down some steps and badly sprained her ankle. She was crying out in pain and our entourage rushed her back to the house, where my mother sprang into action. Instructing them to lie Carol on the couch, she told someone to run and get the 'therapist'—a lady who did massage, believed to be the cure-all in Indonesia at the time. Not knowing any better, we allowed the woman to massage Carol's ankle, which is about the *worst* thing you can do for an acute sprain! The earlier ache turned to excruciating pain after the massage. Carol's ankle quickly swelled up and she was in agony. For the next three days she was bedridden, and for many days after, she was still hobbling.

By now, Carol was starting to feel frustrated. The honeymoon she dreamed of was not turning out as she had hoped. Her only comfort was my mother's beautifully fresh, home-made bread, which she loved. "I thought this was our honeymoon," she said one afternoon while sitting up in bed, her ankle propped up by pillows. "What are we doing here?"

I was at a loss. I had made the mistake of not protecting our time together and had allowed ministry and family to crowd in on what should have been an opportunity for us to connect as husband and wife. Realising my mistake, I knew an apology was in order. I expressed my sincere remorse, and together we decided to learn from this experience. We knew our marriage was for life and were grateful we would have more opportunities for better times together. Thankfully, as I began prioritising my wife's needs over the call of extended family or ministry, the rest of our time in Ambon looked a little different!

CHAPTER SEVEN

Back in Java, the local churches had been waiting for our return and were keen to work with us. We threw ourselves enthusiastically into hosting outdoor evangelistic rallies. The churches promoted our meetings well, and we often had several thousand people attending. Many were non-believers who arrived with a friend or family member, while others came as casual onlookers, curious to see what was happening.

By now, our team had a smooth working rhythm and all was going well, with each rally bringing fresh momentum. One night, however, as the band brought the worship time to an end, I noticed Carol disappear from behind the keyboard. Running off-stage, she then suddenly reappeared a few minutes later looking a little flustered. Wondering what was bugging her, I quickly stopped by the keyboard before taking the stage to speak. "Are you okay?" I asked. Carol reassured me all was well—she just felt a little 'off' and wondered if perhaps it was something she had eaten.

The following day, however, Carol was feeling worse and needed to stay in bed. For the next few days, she remained nauseous and unwell. Our team were asking the Lord to heal her, but as the symptoms were not dissipating, I figured it was time to get some medical help. A quick trip to the doctors revealed, to our surprise, that it wasn't a tummy bug at all—Carol was carrying our first child! We had only been married a few months and weren't expecting a pregnancy so quickly, but we were absolutely delighted.

The idea of becoming a father took some time to adjust to. Thankfully, for the next few months my focus was completely on Carol who found that, in her case, morning sickness was in fact, 'all-day sickness'. Out of concern for her and the baby I suggested that she should take some time out from travelling, but Carol loved ministering with the team and didn't want to miss out on anything. Plus, she said, the travel and ministry helped to distract from the sickness.

We knew that these were significant times. God was using our team to bring His healing and salvation to many lives, and Carol wanted to be in the middle of it all. On several occasions the nausea was so intense that she would race off the platform, be sick over the railing, and hurry back to carry on playing the keyboard. My lovely wife persevered through the sickness over the next few months, touring right up until it was nearly time to deliver.

◆ ◆ ◆

When we were not touring, home was a small house close to the Tawangmangu Bible College. We enjoyed being near Carol's parents and helped out with teaching and administration wherever we could.

One day, a pastor who had a small house church asked if our team would host some meetings. He hoped that many would hear the good news and become followers of Christ. We agreed to this, but as it was the rainy season, we suggested it would be best to use a covered venue instead of our usual outdoor fields. The pastor tried to book an indoor venue, but finding none available, he went ahead and reserved the local soccer field, believing for the best. We knew this was a risky move. Wet season rains in Indonesia are not gentle showers—they are tropical downpours. Still, we could see the passion in this pastor, and we genuinely wanted to help him.

Feeling very unsure about proceeding with the meetings, I decided to check out the field. The wrestle between wanting to help the pastor but knowing the considerable loss of time, money, and effort if it rained was heavy on my mind. I knew that it did not make sense to go ahead with the meetings. I was also aware that if our sound system and musical instruments got damaged by water, they could be irreparable.

However, as soon as my feet touched the grassy field, I felt such a tremendous peace come over me. The peace of God is beautiful—it is the absence of all doubt. This deep sense of contentment allowed my heart to feel free to go ahead with the proposed meetings. I believed that God was giving us the 'green light'.

We started gathering as soon as we received a council permit to host the meetings. The first night, everything went well. Thankfully, there was no rain, and more importantly, people heard the good news about Jesus. Some were also miraculously healed, which piqued people's interest and led to more people coming the next night.

On the second night, the large crowd were enthusiastic. The believers responded by clapping and raising their hands in the praise and worship. The non-believers were enthralled by what was going on. There was an air of anticipation as these simple village people experienced something outside their routine of work, eat, sleep. There was nothing compelling to watch on television—if they owned a television—and smartphones, social media, and the internet didn't yet exist. Our meeting was an exciting moment in the life of the village, and everyone was expectant.

I, on the other hand, was watching the ominous black clouds hovering above us. Before long, the drops started falling, ever so lightly. *Perhaps it will just rain a little bit and then dissipate*, I hoped.

Soon I became more desperate. "Please Lord, make it stop," I prayed. "You gave us the go-ahead, but if this rain continues, we won't be able to carry on."

The rain kept falling, harder and harder, and people were starting to leave. The band was doing their best to keep everything going, but I could see they were unsure what to do.

Stop the rain, Sam.

That was it. Just a feeling inside that the Lord wanted me to stop the rain.

This was new. I've never heard of anyone stopping the rain before. My mind flashed back to the sixteen-year-old boy who had been healed from deafness without anyone praying for him. That was new for me too, and my faith had grown from that experience. Now I realised I was going to need to use that faith for this moment.

"How do I do that, Lord?" I asked.

Moving quickly to the stage, I motioned to the worship leader for the microphone. Thoughts were raging in my mind. What if I stepped out in faith, and nothing happened? It would be a huge embarrassment.

What would they think of God? Of me? I didn't want to let the whole team down in front of all these people.

Stop the rain.

"Is that You, Lord?" I wondered. "How do I know it's not just my thoughts?"

My sheep hear my voice, and I know them, and they follow me.[4]

The verse was front and centre in my heart, and I had no doubt the Lord was speaking. Radical obedience was my only choice—I had decided that long ago. As I intentionally put my faith in His Word for that moment, all logical arguments ceased in my mind. God's Word conquered my raging thoughts and I had full peace, believing that my God could do the impossible.

Taking the microphone from the worship leader, I said aloud, "If Jesus is not the Son of God, nothing is going to happen. But if Jesus *is* the Son of God, you will see that the rain is going to stop."

A mass of questioning faces turned up at me, and time seemed to slow.

Looking up at the sky, I pointed to the clouds and said, "Rain, stop in Jesus' name!"

Immediately, the rain stopped.

Just like God had turned off a tap, it went from rain to no rain in seconds.

There was a brief lull as the crowd realised what had happened. Out of the corner of my eye, I became aware of someone jumping up and down. A policeman standing to the side of the stage had been posted as security for the night. Now he was leaping enthusiastically. "This is the true God!" he yelled, as the revelation of the power of God hit him.

Those who had started leaving the field began returning. Some were mystified, others were laughing, clapping and rejoicing. God had shown His power that night, and we were all astounded by His works.

We carried on with the meeting, and that night and on the nights following, many salvations and healings took place as the Lord honoured that village pastor for his faith and perseverance. As a result, his small house

---

[4] John 10:27

church became a much larger church which is still going strong today.

◆ ◆ ◆

"Happy Birthday to you. Happy Birthday to you . . ." Dal's resonant voice filled the house as he took Carol by the hand and danced her around our living room on her twenty-ninth birthday.

My wife, a mother of one with another on the way, laughed as Dal cracked another joke. It was clear to see just how much Carol adored her father and what a strong bond they shared. The bump in her womb was beginning to show, and Dal patted her tummy, telling her how excited he was about the next grandchild. We only had a quick visit together before Dal left for Solo, our nearest city, where he was due to speak that afternoon.

The fourth of March is Carol's birthday and our wedding anniversary, so it is always cause for a double celebration. Wanting to spoil her daughter, Dorothy had invited us to her house for a dinner that evening.

Towards the end of the meal, we were sitting around the table, talking about the future. Carol had been the leader of the Asaph Band, but with a baby on the way she found it increasingly difficult to keep going. Seeing the writing on the wall, we had recently disbanded, but knew we would remain firm friends, if not ministry partners. Now it was time to focus on a new season.

We were enjoying each other's company when the telephone rang. Carol, who happened to be sitting closest to it, went to answer the call. Several minutes later, she reappeared, concern written all over her face. "Dad's been in an accident," she said. "He's been taken to the hospital in Solo. I'm just going to call and get more details."

Always calm under pressure, and not given to assuming the worst, Carol phoned the hospital and was told that Dal had broken his arm and was very weak. There was no indication of anything more serious. Carol was not concerned. Her father had been on a 'water fast' for the past week, which would account for his weak state. Pain from the broken arm wouldn't help either. Dorothy looked relieved that it was nothing more than a broken bone, and the three of us gathered to pray and make plans to go to the hospital.

Dal had taken one car that afternoon, and a staff member from the bible college had taken the second car into town for supplies. We waited, knowing they were due back very soon, but after about thirty minutes, with no sign of the second car, Dorothy asked Carol to ring the hospital to check on how Dal was and to let him know we would be there shortly.

We gathered near the black Bakelite phone as Carol wound the lever and asked the operator to put her through to the hospital in Solo.

The conversation with the hospital was brief—too brief. When Carol got off the phone, she gave us the news—Dal had died. We were too late.

We could hardly believe it. Half an hour ago, the hospital informed us that Dal had a broken arm, and now he was dead?

I felt the grief as I looked at Carol and Dorothy. Stunned and uncomprehending, they crumbled into the pain as the realisation hit. What the hospital staff had neglected to mention in the first phone call, was that Dal had also broken his neck.

Later we found out that the staff member driving the second car home saw the wreckage of the accident. Recognising the vehicle and guessing what happened, he raced to the hospital. Clearly, Dal needed urgent medical attention, but hospital bureaucracy prevented patients from being admitted without a down payment. The staff member had pleaded Dal's case, promising that the bill would be paid, but his cries fell on deaf ears. Time had had run out for Dal, who was left on a stretcher in the hospital hallway, where he bled to death.

◆ ◆ ◆

We held the funeral the following day. Word of Dal's death spread quickly, and the ceremony was packed with students, staff, graduates, and people from the community who loved and respected Tuan[5] Walker. Everyone was shocked by his sudden death.

As we walked behind the casket toward the burial ground, it seemed as

---

5 Master

if half of Tawangmangu had come out to support Dorothy and the family. I noticed village farmers shuffling in their sandals, business folk who had closed the office for the day, bible college graduates-turned-pastors—the main street was filled with people as the crowd thronged behind his body. All were mourning the loss of a man who had been a friend to many and had brought so much life, joy and love. I felt a deep heaviness as I contemplated such great loss.

Dal was buried on a beautiful site facing pine-studded hills surrounded by vegetable farms. It was a peaceful spot where the prevailing sounds were the wind in the trees and the gurgling water from the river below. As the last of the dirt was shovelled onto her father's casket, I noticed my wife had turned her face to the setting sun. Following her gaze, my eyes beheld a most magnificent sunset. It was as if heaven was standing at attention to welcome one of its Generals home. The verse that came to mind was: "Precious in the sight of the Lord is the death of his saints" (Psalm 116:15).

◆ ◆ ◆

A few days later, Carol and I moved onto the college campus to be with Dorothy. Carol was overwhelmed with grief. She'd had a very close relationship with her father and had looked up to and admired him all her life. Now he was gone, and she felt his absence acutely. In conversation late one night, she told me that with her dad's passing, it was as if the life had gone out of the college. I understood what she meant. Dal had an energetic personality and had been a beloved father-figure to so many. Friendly yet genuine, animated and humble, he modelled humility and Christlike integrity. I had watched him over the years mix easily with people of all ages, stages, and beliefs. His warmth and enthusiasm drew us all in, and he liked nothing more than to be around people and have a good laugh.

Most of Carol's siblings lived overseas at the time, but her younger sister, Glenys, and husband, Michael, were also living in Java, working as missionaries. It was a great comfort to mourn together as family.

Over the next few days as students and graduates flooded in to pay their respects, Carol and I stood by, wanting to lend Dorothy our support, as she cared for the staff, students and alumni who were also mourning. Carol's admiration and love for her mother grew as she saw how strong she was in those moments, and how she extended comfort to others whilst choosing to grieve privately behind closed doors.

In the weeks that ensued, family and friends from New Zealand and America flew in, bringing welcome comfort and distraction to the grieving family. Some of Carol's siblings stayed for weeks, making the most of the opportunity to visit their father's grave and to grieve together, and we were grateful for their presence.

Eventually, the last of the kin left and we wondered what Dorothy would do now. At fifty-two, she was a missionary widow living in an adopted country. Carol and Glenys were her only blood-relatives in Indonesia, but she had other adult children living overseas who would gladly take her in and look after her. Dorothy could easily have packed up and lived the rest of her life in comfort, amongst family.

But my mother-in-law was a stateswoman. God had called her to Indonesia and its people, and that call did not die with her husband. She knew her time in Indonesia was not yet up. Although it was hard, Dorothy chose to put her hand back to the plough and embrace even greater responsibility, knowing that our heavenly Father doesn't exclude the single, the broken, or the weak. All He needs is our surrender and availability, and that is exactly what Dorothy offered.

I was stunned by the depth of forgiveness Dorothy showed. Ultimately, Dal would still be alive if not for the hospital bureaucracy he had encountered. However, just as Christ had forgiven her, Dorothy also extended the hand of forgiveness to those who had withheld the medical attention her husband needed. This is the hallmark of a forgiven person. Her choice to keep serving a people not her own, and to live in a country where, until recently, she had only known financial need, illness and injustice, was a huge testimony of God's grace to all who knew her.

CHAPTER EIGHT

After Dal's death, Dorothy began depending on us more to help with the running of the bible college. I became the dean of men and took on more teaching hours, which I was happy to do. It felt like such a privilege to spend time diving into the Word of God as I prepared for the lectures. This was a significant shift for me after years of ministering as a healing evangelist, but it was an opportunity for me to grow in my role as a teacher, and I embraced it. At the same time an increasing number of invitations came in, asking me to speak in churches around the country. I felt the Lord entrusting me with more as I was faithful with what He had already given me.

Within a year of Dal's passing, my speaking schedule was packed. I was at capacity, lecturing up to twenty hours a week in the bible college, providing pastoral care as the dean of men, preaching at churches on weekends, and regularly speaking in seminars around the country. We didn't own a car, so journeys were mainly by bus or train, and the travel time was extensive. Occasionally I flew to another island, and when this was the case, I could be away for two to three weeks at a time.

Carol continued helping Dorothy with the college administration, as well as looking after all my correspondence, responding to every invitation on her manual typewriter. This meant hours of work for her, and life was generally hectic for both of us. By now, we had a one-year-old and a two-year-old, and Carol was expecting our third child. Thankfully, seeing the need for some balance, she began booking my speaking engagements only every second weekend, so I could have time at home with our growing family.

Still, we had difficult choices to make. Our youngest child had always had difficulty settling and seemed to cry constantly. Normally unflappable, my wife struggled with this, and during one of my longer stints away, it reached crisis point. Feeling she could no longer cope, she sat down and started to write a letter, asking if I could please come home and help her as she was at her wit's end. As she wrote, however, she remembered that we had promised to put God first in our marriage. At this point, Carol felt she needed to examine her motives. Was she writing the letter because she needed help, or because she wanted her husband to be at home? She realised she had many people around her who would readily come to her aid if asked. She also sensed the Lord was asking her to rely more on Him, rather than on me, her husband.

Carol never did send that letter but made the decision to put her trust in the Lord and ask for help from those around her. I admired my wife so much when she told me this on my return home. From the beginning of our marriage, we understood that we were partners in ministry and that neither of us was more important than the other, but we also knew that fewer people would have heard the good news of Jesus or been helped by my ministry if Carol had not been so willing to surrender and obey the Holy Spirit in this season of life.

We never received a salary for my work at the bible college. Instead, our income came predominantly from a church in America who had supported Carol with a monthly cheque ever since she was a single missionary in the Philippines. While it was a generous amount for a single woman, it was barely sufficient for our growing family. The churches where I preached on the weekend were as generous as possible, and sometimes they took up an offering for me, but Indonesia's economy was not doing well, and people didn't have much to give. As a result, the offering money would go towards covering my travel costs—and sometimes it was not even adequate for that.

The economic situation also meant that many of the bible college students from small churches and low-income families struggled to pay their college tuition. At times these students went for months on end without any means to pay their fees or even buy personal essentials. As our college was a full-time boarding school, finding part-time work was not an option for the students. Even if it was, jobs were not easy to come by. Most people in the area were farmers living hand to mouth. Still, the college was reliant on the fees to operate, and we were hugely impacted by slow or no tuition. Often, our whole faculty and students were on our knees asking the Lord for His help and provision in this area. It was at these times that I had to remind myself that just as my heavenly Father had provided several pairs of tailor-made trousers for me all those years ago when I was in bible college, He would also look after my family and all those under my care. That first miracle of provision in my life as a young man was the seed from which my faith kept growing.

◆ ◆ ◆

My faith was about to be enlarged even further when we began thinking about spending some time outside Indonesia. It had been a taxing few years since Dal's death. Now, with the birth of Sheryl, our third baby, we were feeling stretched and needed an extended break. Carol never complained, but she had not been back to New Zealand for years and I could see she was longing for her family and country. We began to make plans to travel to New Zealand so we could spend Christmas with Carol's siblings.

Our proposed trip was a huge step of faith. We had no savings and a meagre steady income, but we began to pray, budget, and save what we could. Having been an itinerant evangelist in my earlier days and now spending much time on the road for ministry, travel was familiar to me. I was not, however, used to travelling with a family of three small children, and having never been overseas, this trip was a big deal for me. There was also the question of what we would do once we were in New Zealand. There was no guarantee that I could get work so we were unsure how long we would stay for. I knew we would require a substantial amount of money, and although I believed God could provide, I realised my faith needed to grow.

One day as we were praying about the trip, I felt deep down that the provision for our travel would come from New Zealand. Carol and I had not told many people of our plans or our lack of finance, so I wasn't sure how this would happen and decided to keep my inkling quiet.

That day, I happened to be teaching about faith at the bible college. This took on a fresh sense of significance as I felt my own faith being stretched! However, as I was preparing my classes God revealed to me that when we receive a word from the Lord, we must grab hold of it and speak it out in agreement. He showed me that when we do this, it changes our unbelieving mindset and grows our faith. The Lord wanted to walk with me and show me His provision, but I needed to come into agreement with Him. I also realised that by speaking out loud, others hear our declaration, and we become committed to it! I began teaching my students that faith is not faith if we are quiet about it and never act on it, and that there is great power when we speak the Word of God aloud, agree with it, and then carry it out.

Knowing I must practise what I preach, on arriving home after class one day I said to Carol, "As we will be going to New Zealand, I believe the money we need will come from there." I didn't know it at the time, but Carol thought to herself, *How will that happen? No one in New Zealand even knows who you are!*

Still, I knew the Lord had spoken to me, and decided to keep my words in agreement with what He had said. As a couple, we had decided early in our marriage that we would never broadcast any lack, or hint about our needs to others. Instead, I started declaring scriptures out loud every day about God's provision over our circumstances. I could feel my faith growing within me. It was as if we already had the finances, even though in the natural, we were a long way off.

◆ ◆ ◆

A month later, a letter arrived from a group of young adults in Auckland, saying they had collected an offering for us and wanted to know if we had any specific needs. Carol wrote back asking if the gift was intended for the bible college or our family. They assured us that they wanted to bless us personally, and were so excited when Carol told them we were coming to New Zealand and needed money for our trip. The young adults insisted that the funds be put towards our travel expenses, and said they would love to meet us and have us visit their church.

We were thrilled at the way the Lord worked! He had moved in the hearts of a group of people we hardly knew, to take up an offering for us! The fact that they were in New Zealand encouraged me and confirmed the word I had from the Lord regarding our travel funds coming from there. Not knowing our circumstances, this group had been obedient, and now, along with the little we had saved, we had enough to book our flights. God had provided for the first step of the journey, and although we still didn't have money to cover our living costs in New Zealand, we needed to move forward, believing He would continue to look after us when we got there.

However, our faith was about to be tried even further. A few days before we were to leave Java, Carol checked in with the treasurer of the bible college to ensure that all was on track with the college funds. "Is this all there is?" she asked incredulously as she scanned the college bank account. We were dismayed to discover that there was very little in the account—enough to last a couple of weeks, but nothing past that. Being the holiday period, there would be no more student fees coming in for a couple of months. This was a huge blow, and I felt the weight of the responsibility. I believed that God had given us the green light to go to New Zealand, yet how could we leave when the school was in such need?

The only money Carol and I had left was the sixty dollars from our monthly support. We were planning to use this for food on our trip and to buy groceries when we got to New Zealand. There was no other income until the following month, but deep in the pit of my stomach, I felt the Holy Spirit nudging me to give what we had. It wasn't a lot, but I knew that once we converted it into rupiah it should be enough to get the college through the month. I argued back and forth in my spirit, telling myself that my family is my primary responsibility, and we needed that money, but it was futile. I knew I had to obey, even though it was a very hard thing to do.

I felt my heart being pulled, knowing that once we gave this, we had nothing left for our family to live on during our first month in New Zealand. I was about to take my family to a country I had never been to before, meeting people I didn't know and who didn't know me. At least in Indonesia I was often invited to churches, and God would provide for us through love offerings, but in New Zealand, no one knew me as a speaker.

    Carol and I talked and prayed, then agreed to put that money into the school account. For me, this was a huge sacrifice. As a husband and a father, this was the hardest thing I had ever had to do up to this point. It felt like we were about to walk into the dark with nothing and nobody on whom to rely. What do you do when others depend on you to lead and provide, but you have no one to turn to and nothing left in the bank? Fear and worry started to creep into my mind. I felt stuck, but the flights were booked, the plans were set, and there was no going back.

CHAPTER NINE

We had found the cheapest flights to New Zealand through a French carrier that transited in New Caledonia. Having never been to New Caledonia before, we didn't know anyone there, but in the course of planning the trip, we learned of a thriving Indonesian community on the island. We managed to get in touch with a kind Indonesian Christian, who helped arrange our accommodation and told us he would pick us up from the airport.

Our trip to New Caledonia was pleasant. We arrived on a warm Friday afternoon in December and the Indonesian man met us at the airport. He cheerfully showed us around the city, then asked if we could pray for his pastor, who happened to be sick. We said we would love to pray for him, and the following day, he took us to visit the minister. After we prayed, the pastor told us he felt God had brought us from Indonesia so I could preach at his church the next day. Feeling honoured to be asked, and happy to help, I gladly accepted.

The church in New Caledonia welcomed us warmly. Many of the three hundred members were Indonesians, and they were keen to hear from an Indonesian speaker. What a huge answer to prayer it was when, at the end of the service, they blessed us with a love offering. We were so thankful to the Lord for this gift! I felt the weight lift off me knowing we would have some money for groceries once we arrived in New Zealand.

The next day, about twenty members from the church came to visit us in our accommodation. They were eager to get to know us better and to hear news from back home. We spent a wonderful afternoon with them, and as they were leaving, they came in single file to shake our hands before exiting. One after the other, as they hugged me goodbye, each person pressed an envelope into my hand. I just stood there, knowing they were blessing me but feeling so humbled. They also gave perfume to both Carol and me. This was the first time I smelt *Kouros,* and it became my favourite scent.

When they had left, Carol and I gathered all the envelopes and counted the money. We couldn't believe how much these people had given. It was such a large amount of cash that we had to take it in bundles to the bank to exchange. The overwhelming generosity, love, and lavish kindness of these believers touched us incredibly.

My heart was overjoyed. God had provided above and beyond what we could have dreamed or imagined, through people we had only just met! The sixty-dollar cheque we sowed before we began the trip had been multiplied many times over before we even landed in New Zealand.

My heavenly Father was showing me yet again that He can be trusted. He had planted a word in my heart all those months ago, and I had watered that seed and allowed my faith to grow. It was not an easy journey to get there, and I had to choose to surrender even when it felt impossible. Now, here we were, standing in a French bank in New Caledonia, with bundles of cash ready to exchange into New Zealand dollars. We had been blessed in the most profound way. The next day we boarded the plane for New Zealand with happy hearts, knowing we could live off that gift for weeks!

◆ ◆ ◆

Celebrating Christmas in New Zealand took some adjustment. Although it was summer, the weather was much colder than in Indonesia, but the starkest contrast was how quiet and unpopulated the country was! I was incredulous when I heard that New Zealand had more sheep than people, but the miles and miles of beautiful green countryside dotted with fluffy white animals proved the fact.

Most of Carol's family lived in Wellington, and we had a fantastic time with them. It was beautiful to see her in her home country, enjoying all the things she had missed while living in Indonesia. She introduced me to all the good 'kiwi' food, and my first taste of New Zealand lamb had me hooked! Everything was different and new.

We rented a small house and enjoyed spending long days together as a family. Having a break from ministry responsibilities and travelling all the time was such a welcome respite. When some family friends who owned a candle factory heard I was looking for employment, they offered me a job in their business. This was such an answer to prayer, and Carol and I rejoiced that we would be able to stay longer in New Zealand. I had never worked a manual job before but found the work to be satisfying and fulfilling. It was a small factory, but the relationship between the employers and employees was excellent, and the staff were very good to me. After just a couple of months, the boss came and gave me a key and told me I could come and go when I liked. I gladly took this as an opportunity to work overtime and earn more for the family. My role was straightforward, and the money was regular. The hardest part of the job was having sandwiches for lunch when I was used to a hot meal of rice, meat, and vegetables!

Life in New Zealand was so easy—everything seemed uncomplicated, and we were comfortable. I enrolled in English night classes at the local college and enjoyed the experience of being a student again. I could see us settling as a family here and staying on, perhaps even for a few years. The idea that I could work part-time and study a degree in English was appealing. This was something I had always wanted to do, knowing it would make me more of an asset to the bible college in Indonesia. Carol was so happy having her family nearby, and our kids could grow up with their cousins and go to good schools. Perhaps I could even speak in churches once I built trust with the pastors.

It was a good plan; however, as time went on and the plan became more of a reality, I began to feel uneasy. Something was not right, but I couldn't put my finger on what it was. The feeling of restlessness went on for weeks, and I began to be physically affected. Night after night, my sleep was disturbed, and I would wake for no reason. During the day, I was tired and had to fight to focus on work and not be grumpy at home. I lost my appetite and was not happy.

I realised that I had lost my peace. I had taken that peace for granted, but now it was gone, and the absence was acute. *When had it left me, and how had I not noticed? Had I become so comfortable that I had mistaken comfort and security for peace, and in doing so, made plans birthed out of convenience rather than calling?*

In tracing my thoughts, it was clear that over the last few weeks, as we made plans to stay in New Zealand, the restlessness in me had grown. Deep inside, I knew I was called to Indonesia, and yet here I was, trying to step beyond what the Lord had given me.

We had been receiving regular updates from the bible college during our time in New Zealand, and all had been running smoothly, but it was about this time that I became aware of the desperation in my mother-in-law's voice as she spoke to us on the phone. She had been carrying the load by herself for nearly a year and was beginning to struggle under the pressure. I knew we needed to go back to help her. Together, Carol and I decided to return to Indonesia, and at that moment, peace returned to my heart.

CHAPTER TEN

During our time in New Zealand, we experienced a wonderful miracle that blessed our family greatly. Our son, Ronn, was two years old at the time, and he became very sick with bronchitis. It was distressing to see him so disturbed, especially at night, by a hacking cough and shortness of breath. Knowing first-hand how awful it is not to breathe freely, I did not want to see my son suffer the way I had with asthma. After several days of keeping an eye on him but not seeing his condition improve, Carol took him to the doctor, who prescribed some medicine. Over the next couple of days, Ronn's condition improved a little. Once we finished the bottle though, the cough resurfaced and there was no long-term improvement—he was still very sick.

A well-meaning family member recommended that Carol take Ronn back to the doctor to get another dose, but we were hesitant. We didn't want him to become reliant on medication. Resolving to ask the Lord for a miracle, we began to pray more intensively, declaring scriptures over our son and trusting the Lord to heal him. We kept praying and quoting verses over him, believing there is power in speaking out the Word of God.

In a matter of days, the difference was remarkable! Even though I believe God uses science and works through doctors, in this instance, his healing was quicker and more thorough than the prescribed medication had been. God had proven His power to us yet again, and we gave Him thanks for healing our son. From that day on, Ronn never had another bout of bronchitis—God had healed him totally and perfectly.

◆ ◆ ◆

With our time in New Zealand coming to an end, Carol began to fret about the children's schooling. Marissa was now four years old, and Carol and I had had several conversations regarding the educational options back home in Indonesia—or more specifically, the lack of options. The village schools near the bible college were very basic, and there didn't seem to be any consistency in the standard of education. We had received reports from our staff who had school-age children that they were never sure if their kids would have a teacher on any given day. There didn't seem to be much accountability on the teacher's part to stick to a schedule. Carol was worried about the situation, and as a dad, I also became concerned. A good education was important, yet we weren't sure how to provide one for our kids.

One Sunday before we left for Indonesia, we received a prophetic word during a church service in Wellington, specifically to do with our children. We were told not to worry about them because the Lord would look after every detail of our kids' lives, *especially* their education. Feeling more positive after such a timely and specific word, we determined to trust that as we served the Lord, He would take care of our family.

Driving the familiar route to visit Carol's sister for lunch later that week, we passed a large building with *The New Zealand Correspondence School* (now *Te Kura*) visible on a sign from the motorway. We hadn't paid it much attention before, even though it was hard to miss, but this day it caught Carol's eye. "I wonder if they might be able to help us?" she pondered aloud.

Several days later we walked into the cheerful correspondence school office and found ourselves immediately surrounded by helpful staff and teachers. They interviewed us, interacted with our children, and took us under their wing. We were so impacted by the warmth of the teachers, the quality of the curriculum, and the offers of support. We walked out of the school that day with books for all three kids and a curriculum for Marissa to start when we got back to Indonesia.

◆ ◆ ◆

Arriving home to Java, Carol got to work setting up a school routine for

Marissa and Ronn. In the mornings she supervised their schooling, and in the afternoons, she worked on correspondence and general administration for the bible college.

As a gifted administrator, Carol could see where systems were needed to allow the college to function more efficiently and grow. She established a filing system and taught the staff how to organise information well so they could access it quickly. She then collected all the lecture notes and created subject manuals for each class. As letter writing was our primary form of communication, she also ensured the standard was raised to a professional level.

In her quiet and efficient manner, Carol brought order and consistency to the operations of the bible college and, in doing so, played a massive part in bringing her parents' vision to life. Watching her, I realised just how crucial the gift of administration is. It is often overlooked or relegated to 'lesser' importance than a more visible gift. People often elevated my effectiveness as a speaker and evangelist, or Dal and Dorothy's visionary gifting, but it was Carol's gift of administration that helped set the platform for us to build on.

As time went on, our third child, Sheryl, started her schoolwork. This added to Carol's load, and I watched as my wife struggled with teaching three children, being a solo parent when I was away, and managing the ever-growing demands of the bible college. She knew she could not carry on at her current capacity, but wondered what the solution was.

While typing a letter to a supporter one day, Carol mentioned how much she missed not being involved anymore in the meetings and crusades she so loved. She longed to be part of the team but was now housebound, with three small children dependent on her. Carol loved our kids, and she wasn't complaining, but she was wrestling with the new season she found herself in and the many 'hats' she had to wear. It was as if there was a constant, invisible tug-of-war between ministry and motherhood.

In her reply, the sponsor encouraged Carol, saying, "Those three children are just as important to God as the thousands out there in the rallies. When they grow up, it is they who will be reaching the thousands!" This was a turning point for Carol. It was as if someone had switched on a light bulb, and she began to see our kids as her new mission from the Lord. My wife was already a great mother, but now she also took on responsibility for their discipleship.

I started to see scriptures go up on our walls and toilet doors, and heard her teaching our little ones scripture memorisation. Daily she would repeat verses to them, and in no time at all, our kids were quoting scriptures. I was amazed! We began to set aside time each night to gather the family around a bible story and a short prayer. As the children grew, I would get my guitar out, and we would sing together. Our children became Carol's new 'ministry', and as she threw herself into it, her attitude went from being resentful to being fully persuaded that the Lord would bless her in this. I admired my wife so much for how she applied herself to this calling, knowing that God had given us these precious children to train up in His ways.

Carol understood that it wasn't a matter of motherhood versus ministry. She knew that one didn't need to come at the expense of the other, but that both should *complement* each other. Motherhood *was* ministry—probably the most important one—and if she could invest wisely, she could, over time, reap on her investment, not once, or even twice, but in our case, four and over!

Although she was buzzing with fresh energy and motivation as a mother, Carol was still juggling the demands of the bible college, and we had to find a solution to free her up. On a whim, she decided to put out a call in our regular newsletter for someone to help with the children. Our supporters would often ask what we needed, and we usually mentioned the need for prayer, finance, or sometimes even people. This time, Carol felt it would be good to ask for something less common—a teacher for three missionary children.

A few weeks later a reply came from a young teacher in New Zealand whose pastor had told her of our request. Marie was eager to come and help tutor our children. She had wanted to get involved in missions but had been unsure how to proceed. Coming to help us for six months seemed like the perfect opportunity!

The church sent Marie over to Tawangmangu and supported her while she was with us. She was such a huge help, teaching our kids every morning so Carol could work at the college without sacrificing the children's need for education and support. I could see the relief on my wife's face. It was a solution that worked for us perfectly. The Lord had provided our first tutor for the children, and we knew He would continue to do so, just as He had provided their curriculum and resources.

By now we were accustomed to receiving big brown boxes of schoolwork each term. Not only were the tattered parcels filled with curriculum but also reading books from the Wellington library for the children to keep. English children's books were a rare commodity in Indonesia, so book arrival day was a bit like Christmas for our avid young readers. Our children had access to excellent education as well as extra resources and books—all free.

Not only that, but over the next eight or nine years, others like Marie came from New Zealand and Australia to supervise our kids, all of them trained teachers. They were outstanding tutors and an incredible gift to our family. We could not have imagined a more exceptional schooling experience for our children and will always be so grateful to the Lord for these women and the churches who supported them while they were with us.

For many of these women, coming to Indonesia was a brave step. Most had never been to a developing country before, but several felt called to mission work, and this was an excellent first experience as they lived in our home and became part of the family. Some stayed for a year or more, and a few returned several times over the years. It was encouraging for Carol to have the companionship of another woman who shared a common background and could talk about things she missed back home, particularly when I was away speaking.

What had started as a problem of too much work for Carol became an opportunity for others who felt called to missionary work but did not have the usual skill-sets in medicine, carpentry, or language teaching. God is such a good Father and provider! He orchestrates every detail of our lives. He's interested not only in our spiritual lives, but in our physical and emotional lives as well.

CHAPTER ELEVEN

My weekend ministry trips became family adventures once we bought our own car. Now that the family could travel together, we would pack our overnight bags, take snacks for the journey, and lay mattresses down in the back of the Jeep. Since there were no seatbelts in cars back then, our young children would happily lie around reading, or play with their toys as we drove along.

We had just finished lunch one Sunday after speaking at a friend's church. Our eldest child, Marissa, was five years old by now, Ronn was four, and Sheryl, the youngest, was three. Seeing them enjoying a game of tag with the pastor's kids, we let them have another few minutes of fun before we all hopped into the car to head home. Everyone was happy, having had a wonderful weekend.

A few days later, Carol mentioned how tired the children seemed. Home-schooling had been a bit of a struggle for the older two that day. The next day, the children were even more listless and kept wanting to lie down. We knew something was amiss, so we decided to take them to the doctor in Solo. Going to see the doctor was never a light decision—we weren't in the habit of driving forty-two kilometres just for a cold or cough—but by now all three children had developed a fever. It looked like they had contracted a virus.

Sure enough on arrival at the clinic, the doctor took one look at the children and immediately pronounced 'Typhus'. After the appropriate tests, it was confirmed that all three children had contracted the disease. Marissa and Ronn were immediately admitted to the hospital. Knowing delirium was a real danger with high fevers, the hospital staff attended to the kids as soon as we arrived, stripping them down and applying cold compresses.

Marissa's temperature was so high that they packed ice around her body to bring the fever down.

Ronn was in the room next door, and there was a glass partition between the rooms so they could see each other, which was a small comfort to us as we were not allowed to stay with them. Sheryl's symptoms were less severe, so the doctor allowed us to take her home as long as we followed her care instructions implicitly and monitored her closely.

It was a tough decision to leave the older two in the hospital. As we walked down the corridor, we could hear Marissa crying and screaming for us not to go. It was heart-wrenching, but there was nothing we could do. Thankfully, this was a good hospital. We knew the nurses and doctors would take proper care of our children, and I promised to come back the next day. Carol and I prayed all the way home, declaring healing scriptures over all three of our children, and asked the Lord to give peace to our older two in hospital.

The following week I was booked to travel to the island of Manado. This weighed on my mind. It wasn't a good time to be away for ten days and I wondered if it might be better to postpone the meetings. Carol assured me, however, that I should carry on with the plan and that all would be fine on the home front. Sheryl seemed to be stable, and we were confident the older two would recover quickly now they were in good care.

Thankfully, Marissa and Ronn improved very quickly. After a few days we were allowed to bring them home, so long as we were consistent with the medications, watched their diets, and kept them in bed. Carol nursed the three children brilliantly, although admittedly, it was a bit of a struggle to keep Ronn and Marissa in bed as they were healing quickly and seemed to have all their energy back!

Feeling more peaceful about leaving, and thankful that the Lord was healing my kids, I packed my bags in preparation for my trip the next day. That night, however, Sheryl's condition began to worsen. We prayed and continued to give her the medicine, while I monitored her through the night so my wife could rest. Seeing how quickly the older two had come through the sickness, Carol was confident Sheryl would soon get better, so we decided to stick with the plan. The next morning, I reluctantly kissed the family goodbye and started on my journey.

Not long after I had left, Carol went to check on Sheryl. She was lying in bed very still, and looked pallid. Her breathing was shallow and fast. Carol touched her hand and was shocked by how cold it was. Her feet were also freezing, yet her head was so hot! All the while, Sheryl lay, eyes closed, her body still. *Too still.*

Carol tried rousing her and calling her name, but there was no response. Alarm bells went off in Carol's mind as she rubbed the tiny hands and feet. Fear began to creep in, and she could feel herself falling into it.

What if?

Carol knew the power that fear could have if she allowed it and she decided there and then not to give in to it. "No," she told herself. "Fear will not have me. God is our healer."

She started pleading, calling on the name of the Lord. Tears streamed down her face. "Jesus, Jesus, please heal my child," she prayed over and over, cursing the sickness and crying out to God for His healing. Unaware of how much time passed, she kept declaring the promises of God as she held tight to Him who was her anchor, but still Sheryl remained unresponsive.

Meanwhile, two hundred kilometres away, I got off the bus and was walking towards the airport to catch my flight, when suddenly a voice said very clearly, "One of your children is going to die."

Recognising the voice of the devil, I said out loud, "The Lord giveth and only *He* taketh. *You* have no right, devil."

At about this time, Sheryl opened her eyes! Seeing her mother's worried face, she said, "Mummy, why are you crying?" Relief washed over Carol as she hugged our little girl and gratefully breathed heartfelt thanks to the Lord.

It wasn't until Carol and I swapped notes that we realised that my encounter had occurred at precisely the time Sheryl was slipping away. It was an attack of the devil against my family, but God was our protector. Carol had resolved to stand in faith and declare God's Word over Sheryl rather than give in to fear. At the same time, I had rebuked the devil, and he had fled. From that moment, Sheryl began to recover, although it took a few weeks to regain her full strength. It had been a very close call, but Jesus had the victory!

◆ ◆ ◆

Several months later, we were delighted to discover that Carol was pregnant again. We were believing this child was going to be another son, according to our desire for two boys and two girls.

It was just over a month from the baby's due date when a bout of frequent earthquakes hit our region. The mountain near where we lived was an active volcano and quakes were not uncommon—this, however, was different. Tremors were happening on a daily basis. Many felt quite strong, and we would find ourselves constantly running out of our concrete rental home to the safety of the outdoors. At night the shaking often caused us to wake and run from our beds, collecting our children as we went. As the days stretched on and we struggled with the broken nights and lack of sleep, we decided to camp out near the front door at night, a move which allowed us to feel a little safer.

Teams of scientists and geologists (some from as far as Japan) had arrived in Tawangmangu to monitor the activity but hadn't found any reason to call for an evacuation. Nevertheless, many villagers further up the mountain than us were leaving their homes and moving out of the area for fear that the next quake would be their last.

It was a trying time, especially for Carol who was already struggling in her late pregnancy with lack of sleep and now had to contend with nerves. One particular night the tremors were so frequent that she couldn't sleep and found herself counting the earthquakes. She got to twenty-four quakes before exhaustion finally took over.

Finally, in a bid to help her get some rest before baby arrived, we booked into a hotel in Solo, hoping that the distance would be enough for her to relax and rest. Carol had a wonderful restful sleep—for one night. The next day, she promptly went into labour.

We were thrilled by the arrival of our fourth child, another son, whom we name Jeffrey, meaning 'divine peace'. Interestingly, the quakes died down not long after we arrived back home with our peaceful baby boy!

◆ ◆ ◆

By now, the older children were keen to learn an instrument, and having been involved in music ministry ourselves, we wanted to facilitate this as much as possible. I began teaching Ronn some guitar chords and he quickly learned how to strum, showing natural talent. Sheryl had a lovely singing voice and good pitch, and Carol began to teach her singing and simple breathing techniques. Marissa wanted to learn the piano, and Carol was able to give all three children keyboard lessons and teach them how to read music. We were delighted with our children's progress and how much they enjoyed learning. They were like little sponges, absorbing all we knew. Before long, however, we had exhausted our limited knowledge and knew it was time to find a more skilled music teacher.

With no music school in Solo, our nearest city, we asked around to see if anyone knew of a good music teacher. There was no immediate response, until one day, there was a knock at our door. I wasn't home at the time, so Carol went to see who it was. On the doorstep was a man who introduced himself as Ronnie from Solo. He didn't offer too much more information, but as it is considered rude in Indonesia to leave people on the doorstep, Carol invited him in.

Stepping into our lounge room, Ronnie spotted our keyboard and asked if he could play it. *That's an unusual request for someone who has just met us*, thought Carol, but she gave her consent, and in a minute, the house was filled with the beautiful sounds of his playing. There was no doubt this man was a gifted musician—and he could also read music! This was not common, as many Indonesians have a musical ear and never bother to learn to read notation.

Seizing the opportunity, Carol asked if Ronnie would agree to be our children's music teacher. She offered to pay for his time and transport costs, and although this man didn't drive and had to take a sixty-minute bus trip each way, he agreed. We were overjoyed!

◆ ◆ ◆

Ronnie came faithfully for a whole year to teach our older children how to play the keyboard and read music. He was so patient and thorough, and they learned quickly under his careful tutelage. A quiet man and not very talkative, our conversations centred around music and the children's learning.

As the end of the year approached, we told Ronnie that we would need to stop the lessons for a few months while we were away in New Zealand on leave. We agreed that he would carry on with the lessons once we returned from our trip.

Three months later, we were back in Indonesia and expecting Ronnie to turn up for the children's music lesson as planned, but the session time came and went, and there was no teacher. We wondered if we'd given him the wrong date. Perhaps he would come the following week? The next week came and went, and still he did not show. We waited another week for Ronnie to return, but he never came back and never got in touch with us to say that he wasn't returning. This was before the days of cell phones, and most Indonesians didn't have a telephone in their home, so we couldn't contact Ronnie easily. Wondering if something had happened, we asked everyone we knew in Solo about him, but no one seemed to know who he was. No church music groups, no music shops, no one at all seemed to know our music teacher.

To this day, Ronnie remains a mystery to us, and we have never seen him since. All we know is that he was so kind and faithfully taught our children. We had asked the Lord for a teacher, and Ronnie had arrived at our doorstep. As a result, our kids were now well on the way in their musical journey. Could Ronnie have been an angel sent by the Lord to fulfil His promise to look after our kids? We do not discount that this is a real possibility.

CHAPTER TWELVE

Nearly a decade had passed since Dal's death and my mother-in-law Dorothy had courageously carried on leading the ever-growing bible college through thick and thin. A petite but strong-minded, diligent woman, her whole life had been devoted to serving Jesus no matter how that looked. Whether through supporting her husband, discipling her eight children, or continuing to guide a group of staff and teachers to lead a bible college campus, Dorothy had put her hand to the task and tenaciously stuck to it.

However, in the past few years, we had watched her health deteriorate; her stress levels were up, and she was not coping with the burden of leadership as well as she had in the past.

I can't say that I was surprised when one day Dorothy approached Carol and me asking if we would take over the leadership of the college. We had already been carrying much of the operational management for several years, and we knew Dorothy could not carry on, but as soon as the request fell from Dorothy's lips, I felt a pang of inadequacy hit me.

Me . . . lead this bible college? I'm not experienced enough. Carol and I are too young. Also, I don't have a theology degree. I need more training.

The negative thoughts came hard and fast as self-doubt set in. Never mind that neither Dal nor Dorothy had any degrees, or that they also once had no experience leading a bible college—my insecurities rose to the surface, and all I could think about were my failings and unworthiness for the role.

We asked Dorothy to give us a month to pray and fast about her request. After all, this was not a small decision, and we knew we had to get the mind of God. That month turned out to be a time where the Lord shone His light on my insecurities and gently dealt with them. He reminded me that my sufficiency was not to be found in myself but in Him. I realised that I would never be enough for all that He wanted me to do, but that I could learn to depend on Him for everything.

Resolving to trust the Lord even more, I felt peace and security fill my heart, but we still needed an answer on whether we should take over from Dorothy. After a month of prayer and fasting, we still did not have a word from the Lord on this. Over the years, various ministers had given us prophetic words about us becoming the next leaders of the bible college, but I knew we had to hear from God for ourselves. When tough times came—as they inevitably would—I couldn't base my decision on what someone else had heard. I believed that if God could speak to others about my life, He could speak directly to me also.

One day as I was working in my office, my eyes fell on a diary I had kept nine years earlier. Opening it, the page flipped to an entry I had written regarding the last conversation between King David and his son Solomon. David had plans to build the temple, but God told him that Solomon would build the temple instead. I had written in my reflections that I felt that one day in the future, Carol and I were to take over the leadership of the school.

In that moment, it was as if I had gone back in time as I felt again the impression on my heart. Nine years had passed since I wrote that journal entry, but I knew that God was speaking to me clearly, and that the prophetic words we had received were simply a confirmation of a *personal word* He had given to me years earlier, but which I had forgotten.

My heart jumped. This was the sign I had asked for! The Lord had spoken, and I knew that He would be with us. As we waited on Him, He had given a word that filled me with a confidence that allowed me to rise. All that was left now was for me to act on what God had said. It was time to step into a new season of leadership.

Relief and delight were evident on Dorothy's face when we told her we would take over the leadership of the college, and we were glad to be able to lighten her burden.

❖ ❖ ❖

For the previous few years we had rented a home a kilometre or so away from the college. Now it was time to move our family onto the bible college campus. Carol got straight to work on upgrading our new home to suit the family, communicating with tradespeople, choosing colour-schemes, and overseeing the project. She loved having the opportunity to create a beautiful home for our family, and the prospect of moving into a newly-renovated space energised us. It felt to us that God was crowning this new season of our lives with His blessing.

Towards the end of the year, Carol and I were installed into our new roles as the leaders of the Tawangmangu Bible College. To my amazement, my trepidation was now replaced with excitement and assurance. God had exchanged my weakness for His own strength and my insecurities for His confidence. As a couple, we were walking into this new venture with a sense of expectation because we knew we were in the centre of God's will for our lives.

Dorothy, now free of her responsibilities, began to prepare to return to live in New Zealand. My respect for my mother-in-law escalated as I watched the pilgrimage of people coming to bid her farewell in the weeks before her departure. Ex-students and staff who were now pastoring throughout Indonesia owed much to her input, leadership, and example. They came in the hundreds to thank and honour the woman who had given so much of her life to serve the Indonesian people.

Looking on, it was evident that this was her home and these were her people, and I knew how difficult it must have been for her to uproot and return to a country she hadn't lived in for so many years. It was also hard watching Carol saying goodbye to her mother, who she had worked alongside for so long, but she knew her siblings in New Zealand would look after her mum, and that it was now time for her to step up and run with her parents' legacy.

◆ ◆ ◆

Several years after Dorothy settled back in New Zealand, Carol and I were confronted with a situation we had known was inevitable. Our children were now approaching the end of their high school years. While education options had greatly improved in our area, they still weren't great. Most of our staff sent their teenagers further away for high school, knowing that the sacrifice of having their children far from them would be worth it in the end. We had prayed for years about this and felt a peace in our spirits about sending our kids to New Zealand to further their learning.

When Marissa was seventeen and Ronn was fifteen, we travelled back to New Zealand to settle them into high school. From there, it would be an easy transition to university if they so desired. The plan was that we would stay with them for a few months, then Carol and I and our two younger children would return to Indonesia.

After several weeks of getting things in order in New Zealand, Marissa came to me and mentioned that she needed a piano. She was preparing to sit her classical piano exams and needed to put in a reasonable amount of practise. During the week, she could rehearse on the piano at school, but on weekends she needed another option. The Baptist church down the road from where we lived had a lovely grand piano, and after hearing about our problem, they kindly allowed her to use the church piano when it wasn't in use. I was grateful for this, but knew it was only a short-term solution.

As a father, I felt so responsible. We wanted Marissa to do well in her exams, but without reliable access to a good instrument she was disadvantaged. I was her father and provider, and this weighed heavy on me as I didn't have the finance to buy what she needed. As her problem became my problem, I did what I always did when there was nowhere else to go—I took it to the Lord in prayer, trusting my heavenly Father to look after us. I knew He loved my daughter more than I did, and that He saw our need even before we knew we were lacking. Just as Marissa's problem became mine, I could, in turn, come to my heavenly Father and give my issues to Him.

Sure enough, about five days later we received a call from our mission coordinator. "There is some money in your account which has been sitting there for several years," he said. "Feel free to draw on those funds for whatever needs you may have. It's your money."

I quickly checked the account to see how much was in there and was stunned to find we had well over one thousand dollars. Straight away we knew what that money was for. The amazing thing was, God had set this money aside for us years in advance of our need.

We promptly visited a particular piano shop on the recommendation of Dorothy, who knew a man that worked there. This man was a Christian who had spent years perfecting his craft repairing pianos in Buckingham Palace for the Queen! He showed us a second-hand *Danemann* which he recommended not only because it was from a reputable British company, but also because it had an exquisite tone.

The piano was decades old, but he had just finished overhauling it and had done a remarkable job of bringing it back to its full potential. We put one hundred dollars down as a deposit, paid the balance within a matter of days, and within a week we were the proud owners of a beautiful piano.

◆ ◆ ◆

It was evident that God was caring for our children, but even so, it was hard to leave Marissa and Ronn. Although we knew that leaving them in New Zealand was the right thing for them, our hearts filled with sadness as we prepared to travel back to Indonesia. Ronn was only fifteen, and although he was mature for his age, I felt a massive responsibility in leaving him so young. The house we had rented for Marissa and Ronn was in an excellent location, being on the bus route for both the kids' colleges, and within walking distance to shops and supermarkets. My mother-in-law, Dorothy, had kindly agreed to move in with them, and we had settled her in, making sure she had everything she needed.

Days before our departure, however, Carol was on the verge of tears. By the day before we left, she was no longer able to keep them at bay. Tears flowed down her cheeks as she went about her tasks, and I knew her heart was breaking. Our farewell at the airport was emotional for us all, and I wondered how the kids would be when they got back to the house with half the family gone. We had parented the best we could to this point—now it was time to trust God entirely with their care.

CHAPTER THIRTEEN

Back in Indonesia, Carol and I threw ourselves into our work. We were so grateful for the college routine, which framed our days and kept us busy. From its inception, Dal and Dorothy had established a pattern of daily prayer at five-thirty in the morning, as well as prayer during class sessions.

We have learned that there is no shortcut to experiencing the power and presence of God, and when we took on the leadership of the school, it was with this conviction that Carol and I remained committed to keeping a solid culture of prayer. We kept the morning prayer meetings and introduced Friday night prayer watches, to pray through the night either in 'prayer chains' or as a group. Our heart was to develop Christian leaders with sound theology and Christlike character who had also *experienced* God's presence and power.

Prayer is common in many of the religions of Indonesia, and is assumed to be a normal part of our lifestyle as Christians. Many churches hosted an early morning prayer meeting before work, so most of our students were accustomed to this. Prayer is of such high value to us. There is no richer investment than the hours we spend with the Lord, waiting on Him, worshipping Him, and in supplication. It may cost our time, but the rewards of intercession are inestimable.

At the college, we have been blessed to experience seasons where corporately we have known God's glory and presence in a breath-taking way. Countless guests and visitors comment on the tangible presence of God on the campus, and we believe that this is a residue from the hours of faith-filled prayer and praise and worship which draws God's Spirit. There are moments where one becomes aware that heaven is touching earth, and the presence of God is made manifest in our midst. In these moments we have experienced supernatural healings—and demonic manifestations.

Demonic manifestations happen when evil spirits meet with the presence of a holy God. Whenever there is a collision in the spiritual realm, there is a physical manifestation. In a culture where there is a high degree of spiritual awareness and worship of many deities, these manifestations are not uncommon, especially among brand-new Christians.

During one of our Friday night prayer meetings, Carol became aware of a disturbance amongst the female students. It seemed to be centred around one girl who was making unusual sounds and was gesturing with her hands. Her friends were trying to calm her down, but she became more agitated with their attention. Realising that she was manifesting a demon, Carol got up to see what she could do to help.

This girl came from the island of Sumatera and was of Batak descent. The Batak believe in, and call on, a spirit called *Singa Mangaraja*, the 'great lion king', to empower them. She was a first-year student, and the new semester had only just started, so we didn't know her history well, but we could see she was currently under the influence of that spirit. As Carol drew closer, the girl, who had been clawing the air, fixed her gaze on Carol. Her eyes were no longer human and soft but were filled with evil and hatred, and her hands were poised in a feline way to claw anyone who came close. I jumped up to help my wife, and together we grabbed her and removed the student from the room so she could not garner further attention. One thing we have learned is that evil spirits love attention and will do whatever they can to disrupt the children of God from praying!

Once we were in the room next door, we cast out the spirit within her, and a few minutes later, we all returned to the prayer meeting. Praise God, the student was completely free! Many years later, we visited this woman in East Kalimantan where God was using her to bring others to Christ, and she and her husband were pastors of a local church. Truly, Jesus sets us free so we can set others free!

On another occasion, while speaking on the power of God's presence, the Holy Spirit highlighted one of the students to me. He was sitting in the crowd, but it was like there was a spotlight on him which I couldn't miss. This student was a former hired killer who had come to know Jesus in prison, felt God's call into ministry, and as a result, was now in our bible college and served on the worship team. While preaching, the Holy Spirit showed me a picture of his heart, which was so hard it looked like a rock. As a past hitman and convict, he had no doubt seen and done many things that had caused his heart to harden. I knew God wanted to do a work in him and felt to call out the hardness of heart, but not in a way that would embarrass him.

"There is a student here whose heart is hard like a rock," I began, and before I could go any further, the student stood up and came to the front, obviously convicted by the power of God. Stopping directly in front of me, he suddenly fell to the ground and began to writhe all over the floor like a snake. It all happened so quickly—one second, he was walking towards me, and the next, he was on the ground groaning, his face contorted as he squirmed.

This was a demonic manifestation, but it was over in a matter of minutes without me having to do anything. God was in the room, and when He is present, demons must leave—they cannot bear to be around Him. The man, now calm, stood to his feet, and as he did so, we could all see the transformation on his face. He had allowed the Holy Spirit to deal with his hardness of heart, and in a moment, he was a changed man. The freedom on his face was so evident it was as if his face was glowing!

We appreciated that this student had a great singing voice, but in the following service, there was a noticeable difference when he sang. We all sensed such a heavy anointing, one that hadn't been there before, making his gift even more outstanding! Just as he had responded quickly to the conviction of the Holy Spirit, the Lord had done a fast work on him. When he submitted to the working of God in the deepest part of his heart, he found freedom and transformation, which in turn allowed him to step into his identity as a son and true worshipper. The newfound love this man had for Jesus was a testament to the Lord's promise to replace our hard hearts with 'hearts of flesh'. He gives us soft hearts so that we can better know Him.

Over the years, we were privileged to experience the tangible presence of the Lord at the bible college. I have felt the glory of God's presence many times before but it would come and go. This time, however, it was as if we were living under a continual open heaven. It was so beautiful as we enjoyed an extended period of unusual closeness to the Lord, and heaven was so near. Prayer times and services that had on occasion felt tedious and long, overflowed with joy and refreshing, and the minutes seemed to fly by. This lasted for weeks.

Around this time, Carol and I began receiving many visits from pastors around our region who came to us for prayer and advice. We spent hours encouraging and counselling these leaders, some of whom travelled several hours to get to us. They often stayed a couple of days, enjoying the presence of God at the college, then going back to their churches refreshed and encouraged.

We saw such a need for these pastors to be equipped and strengthened. Many of them were in full-time ministry, working hard without much emotional or spiritual support. With this in mind, and with the backing of our staff team, I felt led to run monthly pastors' seminars. These were designed to equip the ministers in the region, offer ministry and encouragement, and provide a space to meet and develop relationships with other like-minded pastors. We were also blessed by the manifest presence of God.

One night during worship, the pastor sitting next to Carol turned to her. "My wife has just gone out to the toilet," he said. "Would you mind just seeing how she is?" Carol wondered why he was so concerned about his wife going to the bathroom, but the band was in full swing, and even if she pressed for more details, she probably wouldn't hear him, so nodding in agreement she went out to find the woman.

Carol got to the bathroom and called out the lady's name, asking if she was okay. The woman's voice behind the toilet door sounded jumpy. "I'm fine … I'm okay …" she responded with a keen edge to her voice. "Do you have a plastic bag I could have, please?"

Carol was curious. "I can go and get one for you, but are you sure you are alright here if I leave you?" she probed.

"Yes, yes. I'm really fine. I … I can't believe it. I think God has just healed me." Sniffles were coming from behind the door. "I've been very sick … cancer in my womb." There was a pause as she gathered herself. "I am booked for surgery in a few days to remove the mass, but we've been praying and asking the Lord for a miracle." Her voice was starting to break. "In the worship tonight, I felt something happening in my body, and now I've just passed it. It's no longer in my body. I'm healed!" She had just passed a bloody mass in the bathroom and wanted the plastic bag to take it to show her doctor as evidence!

We rejoiced with this woman as she celebrated the goodness and healing power of God. Her testimony encouraged the other pastors, and we could see the faith rise as the group was strengthened to believe for greater things. The woman never needed the operation to remove her cancer. She was completely healed and continues to faithfully pastor alongside her husband to this day. God is so wonderful!

During another seminar, one of the pastors brought an ex-marine with him. This man was not a believer, but he was on the verge of a mental breakdown and was in desperate need of prayer. Over the years, the man had dabbled in the occult by going to a Muslim priest to receive power. Muslim priests in central Java are not just practising Muslims—many of them mix ancient beliefs and witchcraft with their religion, then 'give' this power to others. This man had received the power and used it to curse people he didn't like, many of whom had subsequently died.

After years of using this power, the devil now controlled him. A prisoner to his own power, he had tried on several occasions to commit suicide, such was the oppression that he felt from the demons within. Now, at sixty years of age, he was going mad, and his sister-in-law, a Christian, had told him he needed to go to the local pastor to receive deliverance. The 'local pastor' was on his way to our seminar and figured this was as good a time as any, so invited him along. The ex-marine was unsure what to expect, but being at his wits end, he accepted the invitation.

As our evening meeting came to an end, I was delighted to discover the man had come to the front of the room for prayer. As I lifted my hand to pray for him, he instinctively covered his face and began to step backwards, away from me. I prayed a simple prayer as we closed the meeting, and the man left.

At the next month's gathering, the ex-marine came back to tell us what had happened the night he had come forward for prayer. He said that when I lifted my hand to pray, he saw a powerful light from above shining down on him. The light was so piercing and strong that he had to cover his face, and he tried to move away from it, but as soon as it hit his chest, he saw an ugly creature coming out from him. It was like a small baby without hands and feet. With a hideous and furious face, it turned to him and said, "I'm coming back to get you." The spirit then left the building, and the man was delivered that very night. He joined the local church and faithfully followed Christ until his death many years later.

In my experience, when we entirely depend on God, His presence can work powerfully—we don't have to help God. I have often sat with people who have evil spirits clinging to them, and when we start talking, they begin to manifest. It doesn't take much more than a simple prayer for them to be released from their demons, not because I'm anything special, but because the presence of Jesus brings their release. Evil spirits are so afraid of God's presence. At Tawangmangu Bible College we teach our students that we can all walk in this power. It has nothing to do with how powerful or spiritual we are—it's the presence of Jesus in us that brings relief to the oppressed.

The seminars were an outstanding success, and for the fifty-sixty pastors and their wives who came each month, it was such a highlight in their calendar. We ate and laughed and gathered around the Word together. It was a delight to see these fine pastors supporting and praying for one another. They would arrive at our door on Thursday afternoon, many of them looking like the weight of the world was on their shoulders, but by Saturday morning they were encouraged and strengthened for their journey.

CHAPTER FOURTEEN

Demonic manifestation occurs in many ways, and on several occasions, people came to the college office, begging us to help their son or daughter who suffered with depression or was suicidal. Usually, they had been to doctors but the medication had not helped much, and after hearing how God had helped others in our college they wanted to know if we could help. Tawangmangu Bible College is not a remedial home, nor do we have counsellors, but we have seen hundreds of students transformed by the power of God through His Word and in prayer and praise and worship.

Once, while I was away on a ministry trip, a desperate mother turned up and asked Carol to take her daughter in. The girl had been jilted by a boyfriend and was so broken-hearted that she wanted to take her life. Exhaustion framed the mother's eyes as she recounted how her daughter was so low that the worried mother kept waking in the night to check on her. Realising this was a high needs case, Carol was hesitant to take the girl in, as it was semester break and we didn't have many staff around to help. However, she agreed the girl could stay for a few days.

That night, Carol and the remaining staff and students, about twenty-five in total, gathered for our regular Friday night prayer meeting to praise, worship, and pray. The worship was simple but beautiful, the warmth of a single acoustic guitar and lilting human voices stretching up to heaven in adoration. The sense of unity and purpose was strong as staff members began to call out to God with one heart in prayer for the nation.

As everyone was engrossed in prayer, Carol felt a disturbance beside her where the young girl was sitting. Looking to her side, she was alarmed to see the girl gnawing at her wrists. Blood was smeared around her mouth and face and was flowing down her arm as she kept biting at her wrists, trying to sever the veins and end her life. Yet again, we were witnessing a collision in the spiritual realm. In such a beautiful atmosphere of worship, the demonic spirit within the girl reacted by telling her to kill herself. The influence on the girl was strong—she needed rescuing.

Together with another staff member, they immediately grabbed the girl's hand to stop her from biting. Turning her attention to the young woman, Carol could see the girl's mind had become clouded. She was listening only to the demonic voices in her head. A few more staff had now gathered and were casting out the spirit of death while the onsite doctor attended to the severed veins. They reminded the devil that Jesus had won the battle at Calvary, He had redeemed this daughter, and she was His! When the girl came back to her right mind, she was spent from the battle, but at peace. She had been set free from the demonic oppression.

On my arrival home the next day, I met the young lady—she was pale and weak, but alive! Eventually she went back home to her parents. She knew she had a journey to wholeness ahead of her, and that there were some patterns in her thinking that needed to be reset, but she grew in strength as she rediscovered her identity in Christ and learned to declare His words of life.

◆ ◆ ◆

Over the years, we have discovered that evil spirits not only torment people, they also reside in certain regions. One such place is a mountain about sixty kilometres from Tawangmangu called *Gunung Kemukus*. This mountain is a Javanese shrine, or 'high place'. Many people go to the temple there to offer ritualistic worship involving prostitution in the hope of gaining wealth, influence, and power. Such evil acts happen on that mountain, and we regularly prayed against the principalities which control that area.

We began to notice that whenever we drove past this area, something would inevitably happen to our car. We started to get punctures, and I wondered if sharp stones on the road were causing this, but there didn't seem to be anything out of the ordinary that we could see. It was happening so much that I began to get a bit annoyed, but couldn't work out the reason for the punctures.

One night, a group of us were driving home in the vicinity of Gunung Kemukus after preaching in a small town about four hours away. Our teenage daughter Sheryl was in our family car upfront with some of the team, and I was in a second car with an elder from the church where we had just ministered.

Our car, which was in the lead, was driving over some railway tracks when suddenly I saw flames burst underneath the vehicle and heard a loud bang as the car came to an abrupt halt. We braced ourselves, but crossed the tracks with no problems, stopped the car, and I got out and ran to check on Sheryl. I was so relieved to see that everyone was okay. They were a bit shaken but had not seen the flames and did not know why the car had stopped. I was glad they had not witnessed what I had seen, as it was a frightening sight. When we looked at the tyres on my car, they were completely burnt, and there was nothing left of the wheels. The fire must have been scorching—even the hub caps were destroyed! I was so grateful that the rest of the car had not suffered any damage.

Borrowing the elder's car, I drove to the next big city where I purchased four new tyres, then travelled back to where everyone was waiting and attached the new tyres to my car before finally resuming our journey.

Several days later, I was driving past the same place. By this time, whenever we approached the vicinity of Gunung Kemukus, I became edgy, wondering if something was going to happen to our car. We didn't think these goings-on were random, but neither could we work out the cause, nor how to stop them.

Sure enough, as I approached the mountain, I started to hear a rattling sound underneath the car. One of my staff was driving, and I instructed him to pull over quickly so we could get a closer look. We happened to pull up right beside a mechanic who noticed we were checking the car and promptly came out to have a look. On close inspection, he found that the bolts of one of the wheels were so loose that it was about to fall off. This was the car that I had just put four new tyres on and personally made sure that they were tightened properly! How could this happen? I could feel my stress levels begin to escalate in frustration.

At that very moment, I happened to look up. There above me was the place sign which read *Gunung Kemukus*. In a bolt of revelation, I realised that the prayers we had been praying were linked to these attacks. The incidents had started when I began to lead our bible college students in prayer against the principalities in that area, and now the Enemy had opened fire on me in retaliation.

As I delved further, asking the Lord what to do, He showed me that the weapon we were to use in this instance was praise and worship. We knew that worshiping Jesus attracts His presence and that His presence is what defeats the Enemy. Evil spirits cannot stay when Jesus comes! As we worship Him, *He* deals with the Enemy, and *we don't have to do a thing!*

There is an incredible story in 2 Chronicles 20. In the midst of a battle, the Lord set ambushes for the enemies of Israel as the Levites sang and worshiped the Lord. I knew we were to do the same. I went home and taught our students that when we worship, the presence of God is made manifest in our midst. We stopped binding that principality in prayer. Instead, we simply praised and worshipped the Lord. From that time on, whenever we drove past Gunung Kemukus, I sang to the Lord, and the attacks stopped. Praise the Lord, we have never had to deal with those attacks again. Jesus has won the victory!

CHAPTER FIFTEEN

One of my favourite mottos is: *Live to give*. As a couple, Carol and I have always endeavoured to make this a way of life. We are so impressed by how Jesus came to give everything. He held nothing back, not even His own life, and the more we reflect and talk on this, the more this pattern is impressed on us.

I grew up in the era of cash and am accustomed to carrying notes in my wallet, which has been helpful when I feel the Lord prompt me to give. It's much easier and more practical to reach into my wallet and hand someone some cash than to ask for their account number, although we do this as well. There have been very few days in my life that I have not felt a prompting from the Holy Spirit to give money to someone—there always seems to be a financial need, and we are happy to share what we have. However, although I am a giver and follow the leading of the Holy Spirit, this is not something I do frivolously. God has given me a good head for numbers, and calculation comes easily to me. Before any cash leaves my wallet, I am aware of how much I have at my disposal to give.

In the early years of our marriage, Carol would see me handing over money whenever we came across a needy situation. Although she appreciated my generosity, she was more often thinking about the new shorts Ronn needed, or the fact that Sheryl was starting to walk and would soon need shoes, and wondered if there would be enough left for our own needs. I'm happy to report that our children never went without; however, I did have to learn to consult with my wife before giving out *our* cash.

Communication and grace are vital when bringing two people of different giftings, personalities, and in our case, cultures, together. Our marriage is a partnership, and together we find so much joy in giving to others, whether financially or through giving of our time, wisdom, and love.

We were giving much time and attention to the pastors who attended our monthly seminars. These were going well, and we could see that the Lord was blessing the group spiritually as the friendships amongst them grew. The testimony of the pastor's wife who was healed of cancer had opened a new ceiling of faith amongst the group. However, over the course of several gatherings, we became aware that a few of the pastors were struggling financially. Even the bus fare to come to the seminars was, for some, a burden.

One of the village pastors who lived close by had a particularly small congregation. When it became apparent that he and his family were only scraping by, Carol and I were compelled by Jesus' example and knew we needed to do something to help them. Although we didn't have much of a surplus in our personal finances, we decided to support them on a monthly basis. This was a big sacrifice for us even though it was not a large amount, and we knew we would need to budget more carefully. When we approached the pastor and told him we wanted to help him financially, he and his wife were so grateful; it was as if we had given so much more.

After several months we could see the difference our small amount made to his family and we rejoiced in this. Our faith had grown, we had managed our budget, and the joy of giving far outweighed any inconvenience or sacrifices made. Even so, we were acutely aware that so many other village pastors were in the same situation. We felt the tension of knowing there were many other pastors in lack and wondered how we could help meet the greater need.

One day whilst reviewing our budget, Carol and I looked at each other and decided to stretch our finances a little more every month in order to help another village pastor. We had been supporting the two village pastors for a couple of months when we received a call from a minister of a large church in Bali. Somehow he had heard that we supported village pastors, and wanted to get on board. This man had an affluent congregation who wanted to give, and they started to send a monthly sum to fund more pastors. Carol and I were elated. Now we could offer help to more village ministers!

Several months later, a couple of pastors from Australia came to visit us. One day as we were all taking a car trip down the mountain, I shared our vision for supporting our graduates who wanted to plant churches. Up until then, graduating students served congregations in any way they could, but we felt that our students needed to plant churches across the nation. Indonesia is a vast country, and there was room for more churches. Our students had excellent bible training, and were spiritually equipped to pioneer. Sadly, many of them didn't do this because they lacked adequate financial backing. Having lived with, discipled, loved, and invested into our students every day for two years, we felt like their 'spiritual parents', and as a result we felt responsible for supporting them until the newly-established church could afford to keep their pastor.

As we talked, I could feel the excitement rising from our two visitors. One of the men began asking lots of questions, and the moment I mentioned that we wanted to support new church planters, he yelled from the back of the car, "We'll get behind that project!" On returning to his congregation in Sydney, he immediately told his people about the village pastors, and as a church, they enthusiastically began to send financial support.

What started with a humble monthly contribution for one pastor's family had multiplied. Before long we were able to send financial support to one hundred and thirty new church planters every month. God had opened our eyes to an area of lack, we had started with what we had in our hands, and as we were faithful, God moved in others to send money also.

Jesus was a giver, and I believe that as His followers and those who share His heart, we also have the gift of giving, not the gift of grabbing. Jesus teaches, "It's better to give than to receive." We have lived by this principle over many years and have found that if we are faithful with little, He will bless us with more so that we in turn, can bless more. We are the channels that our heavenly Father wants to use to allow the blessing to flow to others.

I have learned that we cannot allow our human minds to stand in the way of the abundant blessing of the Lord. It can be easy to harden ourselves to the needs of others, or feel like we won't have enough for ourselves. Every time Carol and I have resolved to give, there has been an initial struggle. We are aware of our own financial limitations, and it can be difficult to make the sacrifice, but we also know that faith without works is dead (James 2:17).

We don't have a recipe for 'super faith'. In fact, I don't believe there is such a thing. Jesus said we only need to have faith like a mustard seed. That isn't a huge amount, yet God can do a lot with a little faith and an obedient heart. Carol and I have had many testing times in our lives, but we have always tried to be obedient, and the awesome thing is, that when we think we'll be living on plain rice for the next week as a result of giving, we've never had to go without.

God cannot be mocked; He is not a man that He should lie. What He promises *will* happen because He will bring it to pass. We will never lack if we live according to His Word and give to the poor and those in need. There have been times, however, when we have had to wait for the Lord's provision.

◆ ◆ ◆

If you've ever been to Indonesia, you will know that taking to the roads is an experience not for the faint-hearted! The combination of overcrowded streets, an excessive number of motorcyclists, and no road rules (at least, not many adhered to) certainly make for an exhilarating journey! Carol did not enjoy sitting in the front passenger seat as she would witness 'near' accidents, which caused her undue stress. Often, she would arrive home with an aching neck and tired shoulders, from the tension of the journey as rickshaws, buses, cars, and motorbikes wove in and out, converging too close to our vehicle. The motorcyclists were particularly concerning. It was common to see whole families on a motorcycle—toddlers squeezed between parents, and a baby strapped to mum's back—all without helmets!

Interestingly enough, these 'near' misses were just that—misses! Given the amount of traffic and chaos on the roads, it is as if there is an invisible choreography to it all, and although there are many close calls, there seemed to be surprisingly few severe accidents.

During one of our trips to Surabaya, I noticed our car was unstable and not handling the corners well. We hadn't had this vehicle for long, and I felt a bit disappointed that it wasn't driving as it should. Unfortunately, once you get a faulty car in Indonesia, there isn't too much you can do but trade it in. Mechanics can do simple jobs, but there is no used car market as such, and car parts can be challenging to come by.

Upon arriving in Surabaya, I swung by a car dealer to have a quick look, and found a beautiful, white Toyota family wagon which was new at that time. I knew it would be expensive, and we probably couldn't afford it, but I also knew we needed a safer car that could fit all our family and, at times, staff members and visitors. Knowing that this was a reliable vehicle, I put my hand on it and claimed it, saying, "Thank You, Lord. One day, I will have this car."

In my heart I was pleading for that 'day' to come quickly. My gut feeling was that our current car was unsafe and that it would soon need significant work. I debated with myself whether we should promptly sell the car or try and keep it for a bit longer, buying ourselves some time to plan and save. However, I came to the conclusion that my family's safety was more important, and once we arrived home from that trip, we promptly sold the car and began to pray and believe God for a new vehicle. In the meantime, I had to be content with public transport and rides from friends.

A few weeks later I was in my office when I heard some visitors at the door asking for me. My office was located in an upstairs extension of the building, overlooking the entrance to the bible college, and it had a lovely view of Mount Lawu and the surrounding mountains. In the afternoons when it was hot, I would open all my windows to let air through. This also meant I heard all the comings and goings!

Making my way downstairs, I arrived at the front door where a staff member introduced me to a middle-aged couple standing there. After some initial small talk, the wife said, "Pak Sam[6], we came because we felt that you require finance for something."

Not knowing these people, I decided to probe a little further. "Do you mean a bible school need or a personal need?"

---
6 Mr Sam

"For you and your family," they responded, to which I nodded in affirmation. She explained that her brother-in-law had owed them money, but had repaid his debt that morning. As he handed the cash to them, they heard a voice saying it wasn't for them to keep but was for "my servant Sam Soukotta in Tawangmangu."

Although they had never met us, they had heard of us and knew we were leading the bible college. They were prompt to obey the Lord, and here they were two days later, handing over a considerable sum of money. This enabled us to buy a new Toyota, just like the one I had asked the Lord for when we were in Surabaya!

Once again God had shown us that when we look after the poor, He will look after us. We didn't give to the needy pastors intending to receive, but sacrificed willingly out of compassion and in obedience to Him. God's provision of a car was such a blessing to us, but the truth is, Carol and I had experienced even more joy in giving than in receiving.

CHAPTER SIXTEEN

Over the decades a sovereign move of God had taken place in Indonesia. Pentecostal churches across the country experienced great growth, and many young people sensed the call of God and wanted to be equipped for ministry. We rejoiced as we saw rising numbers in the bible college, including many who were new to the faith.

Sound bible teaching coupled with robust structures and efficient work practices meant that our reputation had grown as the pre-eminent bible college in Indonesia. By now we had students from all over the nation and were running a two-year course. There was such an ethnic mix—from the dark and athletic people of Irian Jaya, to the raucous and fiery Sumatrans, the gentle, softly-spoken Javanese, the fair-skinned academic Chinese, and everyone in between.

With two hundred and thirty live-in students, a growing wait list, and no room to move, the college was at capacity. We were renting houses off-site to accommodate the growth, but knew we needed to build another dormitory and had been praying into this. We had enough land to create a new two-storey building that would accommodate the overflow of students and allow for more staff rooms, so we decided that now was the right time to start building our second women's dormitory.

One day, in our early morning prayer meeting, I felt to encourage everyone to be specific in our prayers. We needed approximately six thousand dollars to begin laying the foundation, so we spent a few moments praying into this, and then I closed the meeting. As we walked up the path to our house several minutes later, I heard the phone ring. We quickened our pace, and Carol got inside and answered the call just in time. The caller introduced himself as the pastor of a church in Wellsford, New Zealand.

We didn't know the pastor and had no idea where Wellsford was, but he said, "I'm sending my son and a builder from the church with some money to help build the new dormitory." Carol was so surprised you could have knocked her over with a feather! We wondered how on earth he could have known about this. The only people who knew we wanted to build another dormitory was World Outreach, the mission organisation we had served under for many years. "Wow," gushed Carol, "God answered that prayer quickly!"

The following verse came to mind:

> *Call to me and I will answer you, and will tell you great*
> *and hidden things that you have not known.*
>
> Jeremiah 33:3

We had called on the Lord just ten minutes' earlier, and He had answered our prayers!

A couple of weeks later the builder and pastor's son from Wellsford arrived with money for the building as promised. Amazingly, they bought the exact amount that we had prayed for in our morning prayer meeting! Heading straight to the bank, we excitedly waited as the banker changed the bills from New Zealand dollars to rupiah. When she came back, she told us that we had come on a good day because the exchange rate was extremely high. The favourable rate meant that we received *seventy percent* more than we had initially calculated! We were absolutely stunned! God's goodness to us felt overwhelming, and our guests were thrilled to be part of this unfolding miracle.

Back then, there were no credit cards, and cheques weren't standard in Indonesia at the time, so the banker handed us cash—lots of it! My guests and I were just grinning from ear to ear when we walked out of the bank, not realising what we must have looked like. Carol, who had been waiting outside, burst out laughing at the sight of each of us carrying *two* black travel bags, each stuffed with Indonesian rupiah! She said it looked like something out of an action movie—all that was missing were the black suits, sunglasses and the getaway car!

We made fast progress on the building with that first instalment of money and then kept on praying and building as the funds came in. Today the Hebron building stands as a testament to God's faithfulness. It has housed several thousand students over the years, and has accommodated many bible classes and even a library at one stage.

One year after the phone call from the pastor in Wellsford we were in New Zealand on leave and went to visit the church that had supported this build. The pastor invited me to go for a walk with him, and as we walked on one of the beautiful beaches nearby, I took the opportunity to ask him how he had known that we had wanted to build a new dormitory.

He told me that their church had felt to take up an offering for an overseas mission, but they didn't know who needed it. He had called a mission organisation, and they named a few countries where there were needs, but in his spirit, he didn't feel drawn to any on the list. He then rang our mission's headquarters, who told him which projects needed finance. As soon as they mentioned Tawangmangu Bible College and the proposed dormitory build, the pastor knew that was where the money was to go. We marvelled at how God moves people to accomplish His purposes. Geographical borders and differing time zones are of no consequence to Him.

◆ ◆ ◆

Stewarding the college's future required not only the construction of new buildings but also maintenance of the old ones. Over time we began having lots of problems with some of our older buildings. Being of a more practical nature than me, Carol was very concerned about the leaky roofs and haphazard electrical work. The original electrics around the campus had not been installed well from the start and were now coming undone, with wires and cables everywhere. Coupled with the leaky roofs, this was a recipe for disaster, and we knew we needed some expertise to help with this. There were few skilled technicians in Tawangmangu, and Carol didn't want to call on the handymen she usually brought in. They were intuitive fix-it men who were good with the smaller jobs but didn't have the technical know-how for larger scale projects. With no one local to help, Carol started asking the Lord to please send some men who knew what was needed to fix our facilities.

Shortly after this, a pastor in Sydney asked if one of our alumni, a young lady who had just started pastoring, could come to Australia to give her testimony at their church missions conference. While in college she had been supported by their church, and now pastored in a small village and was seeing great results. Carol wrote back and told him the young lady would love to come, but enquired if they had anyone in the church who could interpret, as she didn't speak English. "No," the pastor replied, "but if you can come with her, we'll pay for your fare too."

A couple of months later, Deborah and Carol were in Sydney, attending the missions conference. Deborah was ecstatic to be overseas for the first time, and both women were so blessed to share at the meeting where Carol could translate Deborah's story. At the end of one of the sessions, a man came up to Carol to ask more about the bible college. He specifically wanted to know whether any building or labouring projects were underway. He explained that he had a team consisting of plumbers, builders, and electricians who wanted to give their time and skills to help in a mission's context.

This was precisely what Carol had been asking for, and she just about laughed out loud! Her heart leapt, knowing that God had answered her prayers. She explained how we certainly needed practical help and would be so happy to have them come.

In due time, a team of six tradesmen from the church arrived at the bible college. They were so helpful, and their work was excellent! They fixed the leaks in the roofs, did a complete overhaul on the electrics, and even built a water tank in their spare time!

This team came back several times over the next few years to maintain our facilities and work on new projects. They were so generous with their time and energy, working alongside our staff and the local tradesmen to pass on valuable skills and knowledge. For Carol, this was a specific answer to her prayers. How encouraging it was to see that God cares as much about the practical aspects of the ministry as He does the spiritual!

CHAPTER SEVENTEEN

Our family life was a joyful experience that Carol and I had relished with our four kids, but all too quickly this season had ended. One by one they had left to study overseas and most recently Jeffrey, our youngest had joined his siblings in New Zealand for his final year of college.

The house felt empty—the vacant rooms were daily reminders of their absence. I missed the kids so much it was painful, and I struggled with the loss. I was a father, but my children were not around for me to be a father to them.

One day, a thought that had been occupying my mind spilled out. "Shall we take some kids in?" I asked Carol. "We have empty rooms. We could foster three children and provide a better life for them."

Carol was also missing our kids terribly, and the idea appealed to her. We mulled it over for days, praying, and talking it through, but we knew it wasn't going to work. This was a busy season of our lives; we were travelling a lot and when we were home, we didn't have much time to give. To take in three young children and then not be around for them was unreasonable and we both knew it.

Perhaps due to my unhappy childhood, there was a longing in my heart to help give children a better life. God had put this desire in me, but for now it seemed, there was no expression for it.

◆ ◆ ◆

Around that time, we heard that an Islamic training centre—proposed to be the largest of its kind in southeast Asia—was going to be built in West Kalimantan. Many of our church planters served in this region, and they knew that if this project went ahead, it would restrict their movements and inhibit church growth just as they were beginning to make headway. As prayer requests came through regarding this, we began to pray persistently into the situation.

The Islamic training centre was an initiative of the Indonesian government at the time, and was proposed to be built in the small town of Balaikarangan, about half an hour's drive from the Indonesian-Malay border. This was a strategic move as Balaikarangan was easily accessible to Malaysia, Brunei and other southeast Asian countries. Until now, West Kalimantan had not been high on the government's aid list and was one of the most impoverished areas in Indonesia, perhaps due to the dense rainforest that separated it from the rest of the country.

Indigenous Dayaks populated the region. They were known as fierce tribal warriors. Traditionally animistic, they practised head-hunting and were feared throughout Indonesia for their reputation of being strong in the black magic arts.

The predominant church in West Kalimantan was the Catholic Church which had been established many years earlier, however, these churches often had no priest and as a result, no significant presence in the local community.

Apart from Dayaks and Catholics, many fanatical Muslims from Madura had transmigrated to Kalimantan, bringing their religion and customs with them. The Dayak people hated these migrants because although they lived on Dayak land, they were not respectful of the indigenous people's way of life and were introducing their own culture and traditions, which threatened the long-standing traditions of the locals. The Indonesian government did what it could to promote peace between the two groups, but there was much ongoing tension, and we often heard of violent outbursts, causing us to cry out for God's peace and protection for those affected.

Ishak was one of our church planters who lived in this town. He led a small house church that had recently started to grow. Ishak himself was a Dayak who had been radically saved and had committed his life to sharing the good news of Jesus Christ with his people. There had not been much headway in Christianity in the area, so the fact that he was seeing growth was an encouraging sign that God was moving in people's hearts.

One day the army sergeant for the area, who had heard about Ishak's church, came to visit him and told him that he would have to leave the town because Balaikarangan was going to become a centre for the Muslims and they didn't want a Christian presence there. Even though Ishak respected and prayed for the leaders in his community, he knew God had a purpose and plan for the Dayaks and he wanted to partner with God in this. He emphatically said to the man, "I am a Dayak. No one can tell me to get out of here; this is my land!"

Several months later, hostilities between the Dayaks and the *Orang Madura* escalated, and tribal warfare broke out. Hundreds died, and thousands were displaced as homes burnt to the ground. The three main representatives who had come to the area to set up the Muslim training centre were killed as a result of all the fighting, and so the training centre never eventuated. God had other plans which we were to be involved in, but we didn't know this at that time!

◆ ◆ ◆

Shortly after the uprisings in West Kalimantan, I received a call from our church planters in the area where the wars had been. About thirty of our ex-students who happened to be working under a Christian organisation were having significant problems with the leadership, and the situation had come to a stalemate. They asked if I would be willing to come over and help them work through this issue.

Carol cleared my diary for a few days, and I flew over to meet with them. It was the first time I had been on this side of Kalimantan, and I was struck by the vast land size of untouched forest and how remote it was. There are no roads or railway tracks across the island due to the highly dense rainforest. After a couple of flights and several hours' drive, I arrived and was warmly greeted by the group of pastors. Having been part of our bible college for several years, they looked upon me as their spiritual father, and to me, they were sons in the faith. We gathered in a very simple house, sitting cross-legged on the dirt floor, and talked through the problem. After a few hours, we started to make good progress as the Spirit of God gave us wisdom.

At one point we took a short break, and I had a few minutes to stretch my legs and survey the surrounding area. Most of the handful of houses were the same as the one we were in—wooden slats with rickety roofs, set amongst a backdrop of dense greenery. Across the road there was an overgrown bushy patch of land which my eyes flicked over briefly, when suddenly, I saw a vision. I had never had this type of vision before; it was like watching a movie on a high-definition television screen. The picture was perfectly clear, even down to the fine details. It was as if I had been transported to a different place entirely, it was so real. Instead of the overgrown jungle, potholed road, and shabby houses, I saw an expansive and manicured complex with many new, lovely buildings on it—some a couple of storeys tall. The landscaping and gardens were beautiful and lush. Everything about the place was tidy, well looked after, and peaceful. As I looked further in, I saw a fishpond with some green plants growing on top of the water, something I'd never seen before. The vision lasted only a few minutes but the picture was seared in my mind, and not knowing what it meant or what to do with it, I kept it to myself.

We ended our meeting, and with God's help we were able to resolve the situation. The next day I flew back to Tawangmangu and started to seek the Lord about the meaning of this vision. As I waited on God in prayer I felt a still small voice saying, "Build." That was all I heard. I did not receive any further details and did not know what to build or where.

In my experience, when God says something, He expects action, which is tricky when you don't have much to go on, but at times like this I keep asking Him for further guidance and keep my antennae up for more clues to act on. I have discovered that when God asks me to do something, sitting back and acting nonchalant is not an option if I want further revelation on the assignment at hand. There must be an engaging, or *leaning in* of the spirit, into that word, which in turn involves my mind and eventually triggers a physical action.

THE SOUKOTTA STORY

In this case, I had captured the word 'build' in my spirit and was mulling over it in my mind, when a few weeks later a man in East Kalimantan contacted me and offered five hectares of land to build a bible college. He wanted to work with us and asked if I could fly over and meet him at the site to look over the land together. I jumped at this, thinking perhaps it was the answer to the vision God had given me.

When I arrived the man drove me to see the land, which was a good section. But although I was hoping it was right, I didn't get the 'go ahead' from the Lord in my spirit, so I refused the offer and flew back to Java feeling a little perplexed. On the flight back, I processed what I knew.

God had asked me to build something.

To do this, I needed land.

It didn't seem to be in East Kalimantan, but perhaps because I had received the vision on West Kalimantan, that's where I was supposed to look for land?

This seemed like a logical conclusion, so on landing back in Java I rang Carol and told her I needed to buy a ticket to fly back, only this time, I needed to head to the west side of the island. There is currently no direct way to get from East to West Kalimantan; to fly from one side of the island to the other you must first fly to Java.

Carol was supportive as always, so I bought the ticket and promptly boarded another plane. Two and a half hours later I landed, and was met by a graduate of our school who proceeded to tell me about a good piece of land nearby which he thought might suit our needs. The land was in Balaikarangan, which I didn't know anything about at the time except that Ishak served there and that this was the general area where the Muslim training centre had been proposed. The village seemed to be little more than a small, dirty market town with messy shops and rough roads filled with potholes.

We drove to the area, and I surveyed the land that the graduate pointed out to me. Bushes covered the entire site with many native rubber and bamboo trees growing on it. It was situated about two hundred metres from the main road leading into the village, and there was also a spring spouting beautiful clear water. We stepped out of the car, and I started to walk towards the land. In my mind, I was having a conversation with the Lord. *Could this overgrown section become the beautiful complex that I had seen in my vision?*

"Is this the place Lord?" I asked. As soon as I stepped on the property, I felt the peace of God come into my heart, and I knew straight away this was the land the Lord wanted me to buy.

We promptly went to see the landowner and asked if he would sell his land to me. He responded affirmatively, and when asked the price, he quoted approximately fifteen hundred dollars for five hectares. I shook his hand and told him not to sell the land to anyone else—I was going to buy it. We did not have the money to purchase this land but I knew it was what God wanted me to do, and my actions had to align with that.

Before we parted ways, we spent a few moments getting to know one another with a little chit-chat. I asked about his family, how many children he had, and what religion he was, to which he responded that he was a Roman Catholic and he had eight children.

"Four of them are Christians, and four are Muslim," he said.

Thinking that it was a bit unusual to have different religions amongst the children, I asked him why this was. He explained that he was a poor man who could not afford to send his kids to a good school, so in order to have a quality education, his children were sponsored. Half of them were financed by Muslims, went to a Muslim school, and adopted the religion. The other four children had Catholic patrons, went to a Catholic school, and grew up as Christians. This seemed to be a common practice in the area.

As soon as the man explained his situation, I knew what the Lord was asking me to build. It was a school! God wanted me to raise a Christian school for the children in the region.

◆ ◆ ◆

Several days later I was on my way to Surabaya to preach. As I was going to collect my luggage from the carousel, I bumped into a Chinese man we'd known for many years from our ministry trips to the area. He was a successful young entrepreneur who the Lord had blessed in his business ventures.

We greeted each other, and he immediately asked if I had any projects that I was working on. His directness surprised me, but I said, "Yes, I have." When he asked me to explain the project, I told him that I wanted to build a Christian school for Dayak children.

He then proceeded to ask if I had found the land for this.

"I just got back yesterday from seeing a large plot of land for sale," I replied.

"How much do they want for it?" he queried. I told him the price and his immediate response was, "I'll buy it for you!" He asked for my bank account number, which I gave him, then hurried off to catch his flight.

Now this may sound pessimistic, but I did not jump up and down or celebrate God's provision then and there. I was excited at the man's offer, but having been in ministry for many years and having received promises of help but not always seen the evidence, I went home and prayed and waited. After a week, I went to the bank to check my balance and joyfully discovered the money from the man had come in as promised! God had given the vision, and now He was providing the finance to buy the land. I knew we were about to get involved in a new assignment, and I was enthused!

I began pondering on a name for the project, and one day while I was praying, the Lord pointed out that the land we had just purchased was sitting at the base of a small hill that the locals called the 'Hill of Fever'. I didn't know the background of this name, and even though we asked the locals, no one could enlighten us about it. We didn't want sickness and suffering to be synonymous with our project—we wanted a name for our school that would give children and families hope for their future. We decided 'Mount Hope' would be the school's name, and in so doing, we declared that this project would bring hope to the hopeless.

❖ ❖ ❖

Before we could start building we had to clear the land, which was an enormous task as we were starting from scratch on a section of land covered with native bushes and trees. When I say 'we', I mean Carol, our staff, and whoever we could get to help. It was a joy to also be joined by the group of men from the Sydney church who had helped us with the bible college maintenance. On hearing about the new project they had jumped at the opportunity to come over to help build a school, and we were delighted to have their support.

The day that we were to start clearing we arrived at the section, and Carol and the Australian group were surprised to find that we did not have any industrial machines or equipment—or even garden tools to work with. The realisation that we would have to start from scratch and do it all by hand caused a small degree of trepidation as we surveyed the abundant overgrowth. Happily, at that moment, all our former graduates from the surrounding villages turned up to help! We were so happy to see them and to feel their support. Their excitement for the project was infectious, and we were elated by their enthusiasm and willing hands!

The temperature on that first day was high, and with the humidity over eighty percent, we were soon all dripping with sweat. Working in the sun in the middle of the day was such hard work that Carol nearly fainted. She had not had a good sleep the night before. Our accommodation was at the only motel in town, but it was old, run-down, and very dirty, and between the cockroaches and lumpy mattress, it had been a restless night. Still, we would not let the lack of energy or lack of correct tools stop us. We had no gardening gloves, and no funds to hire machines or diggers, but we did have lots of enthusiasm, a big vision, sharp sickles, and large knives—compliments of the church planters—with which we started to clear the section. It was strenuous labour. The bamboo bushes were the hardest to pull out because the roots were so invasive; just when we thought we'd got it all, there was still more to remove. We were physically exhausted, but our spirits were buoyed by the church planters who kept singing as they worked, and in doing so encouraged the rest of us.

It was a momentous occasion when, at the end of the day, we stood back and surveyed the work. We had cleared enough land to build our first building, and we were drained but elated. The vision God had given me had now become a vision shared by all those who had laboured with us that day.

CHAPTER EIGHTEEN

As news spread about the new school, small donations of money began to come in and we were able to commence building. Some business friends suggested that we meet with other business people to spread the vision and raise funds to start the school. We took their advice, and I spoke at a couple of these meetings to get the ball rolling but didn't carry on as it wasn't how I generally like to operate. We have always believed that if God gives a vision, then He is the One who will also provide, and in my experience, He has usually done this through speaking directly to individuals.

One day I received a call from the man who had given me the finance to buy the land. He asked how the project was progressing and then said he would send the equivalent of forty-five thousand dollars to start building. This was a tremendous amount of money! I was thrilled to hear that the Lord was blessing him so greatly, and thankful that he was able to sow generously into our project. His money enabled us to construct our first building, which housed the school office, a meeting room, three bedrooms, bathrooms, a kitchen, and an outdoor dining area. It was completed in a few months, and Carol and I stayed there on subsequent visits, which was a much more pleasant environment to sleep in than the local hotel.

Where there once was an overgrown section of land, our first building now stood. We were in the throes of the Asian financial crisis, but still the work did not stop. Steadily and surely the building was completed, and a second building intended as a dormitory was well underway, with no sign of lack.

One day during the building project, a truck turned up out of the blue with a stack of beautiful hardwood. On hearing about our school, a Christian businessman wanted to contribute the best of materials. We had never met this man, neither had we thought to ask the Lord for expensive wood, but this is our heavenly Father! He is into beautiful details and likes to provide the best for His children. We used this lovely wood on the ceiling and the floors, and even today, when people come, they comment on the beautiful wood ceiling.

It was amazing to see God providing so abundantly, and as word about Mount Hope continued to spread amongst Christians, more donations came in. Knowing how much this school was needed in the area, people wanted to contribute towards the building fund.

Having spoken with many locals, we knew that children would come to our school from considerable distances, so we made sure our second dormitory was big enough to house thirty-six children. During this phase we were also able to construct a kindergarten.

As we stood to dedicate the school, our hearts were bursting with pride. I wanted to shout out loud, "Look what the Lord has done!" Where there had been nothing, now stood something. What once was an empty, bush-covered section in front of a hill synonymous with sickness was now a complex with new buildings on the slopes of a mount called Hope!

God had given me a vision and one word, 'Build', and I had simply been obedient to do the groundwork. He had provided all that was needed.

God has repeatedly shown us that our economy is not His economy, and if we are submitted and obedient to what He asks, then we can live by the laws of the Kingdom of Heaven. The Mount Hope land and buildings are a testament to this.

◆ ◆ ◆

Several weeks after completing the first dormitory, we were made aware of the plight of three small children living in the jungle, fending for themselves. We didn't know all the details but came to understand that their father had died several years earlier, and the mother, who was not in her right mind, was unable to properly look after them. At seven years old, Joli, the eldest, looked after her two younger siblings, six-year-old Tanti and five-year-old

Yogi, feeding them whatever scraps she could find. The children spent most of their days foraging in the jungle for edible vegetation. The extended family would take turns giving them food when they could, but they were also penniless and had their own families to feed. They could not take full responsibility for the three siblings, and hearing that we were building a school, they brought the children to us, begging us to take them.

When Joli, Tanti and Yogi arrived they were ragged, skinny, and noticeably unkempt. Their clothes were threadbare and dirty, their hair straggly and unbrushed. *I know there is injustice in our fallen world,* I thought, *but how could this happen to such little children? How could they have survived till now with such little care and so much neglect?*

Our school was not operational yet and the classrooms were still being built, but we had room to house them, and staff to look after them, so we welcomed the three children—glad for God's timing with the completion of the new dorm.

The siblings were not used to living with people and didn't know how to act normally. Having no stable adult in their lives, they had not been taught how to behave or look after themselves. I stood back watching as Carol and others in our team tried to converse with them, but they huddled together and shied away from anyone who spoke to them. They didn't talk much, even to each other, but whenever they did, it was in the local dialect, and we realised they were unable to speak Indonesian fluently—something we had not encountered for many years. The children were painfully shy, and Carol began to worry about how we would look after them if they were fearful of us.

Fortunately, one of our staff was Dayak and spoke the local dialect fluently. When she started to talk to the children, they looked at her, and we could see they could understand what she was saying. Over the next few days, the same staff member kept speaking to them, telling them they would stay with us, that we would look after them and they didn't need to fear us. Very slowly the siblings began to communicate back, and trust started to build between them.

Mealtimes were challenging, however. The children weren't used to eating around a table, let alone with others. As a staff team, we all ate together in the communal dining hall, and even though we weren't a big group, the experience was overwhelming for the siblings. They held back, Tanti and Yogi peering out from behind Joli, all three tentative and cautious. They could see the table laden with steaming rice and fragrant curry, but they would not eat. Although their bodies had undoubtedly adapted to meagre amounts of food, I knew they must be hungry. They were so skinny, and needed to eat soon. Carol suggested to one of our staff that they may be better off eating on their own rather than with the larger group. Happily, this seemed to work, and when the food was taken to their room, the children relaxed and began to eat, clearly more comfortable in their own company.

Little by little, they settled into a routine and started to become more relaxed with us. Although they were still terrified by strangers, we were relieved to see that their wariness around our staff was easing, and we were able to start teaching them to read and write. It was a huge reward to see them progress and, over time, begin to act like normal children.

Word spread that we had taken the siblings in, and before long, other villagers were bringing children to us. Some were orphans who had no extended family to reliably look after them. Others came because although they were able to look after their kids, they couldn't afford to send them to school and hoped that we would educate them once the school was functioning. Then there were the ones who came from impoverished homes, the parents who brought them looking worn and desperate as they shuffled down the drive carrying invisible burdens of worry and shame. These were the ones who did not even know where their next meal would come from. The parents, their faces lined and old before their time, begged us to look after their offspring. For them, it wasn't a matter of education but survival. They brought us their young for the basic need of food and shelter. I felt sadness for these families' situation, but at the same time, I was so, so grateful that we could help them. There was lack all around us, but I could see God's hand working to bring about a future, and in a very real sense, hope, to the families in the area.

One day, not long after we completed phase one of the building project, we headed to the markets with one of our church planters. Having only driven a few metres off our driveway, he turned and queried, "Do you remember how the Muslims wanted to build the largest training centre in Southeast Asia?"

That was several years ago, and we had been very busy since then, but yes, we did remember it. "Yes, we prayed much about that," Carol responded, nodding affirmatively.

Pointing to the section adjacent to our driveway, he went on to say, "That is the land they were going to use to build it."

Carol and I sat stunned as we took in what he was saying to us. The largest Muslim training centre in south-east Asia was proposed to be built on the land next door to where Mount Hope was now situated!

We thankfully praised the Lord that even though others may have had a plan for the area, God's plan prevailed, and where the Muslim training centre would have been, was now a Christian school. I could just see our heavenly Father sitting in heaven enjoying the look on our faces as Carol and I mused over this ironic discovery; I could almost hear Him chuckle at our delight.

◆ ◆ ◆

Once the first few buildings were complete, staff from Tawangmangu Bible College came to help get things up and running as we prepared to launch the school. Abraham and Melanie, who had first come to the college as students and were now staff, made the trip over with a few others. They were delighted to see Mount Hope, having prayed about it with us at the college for several years. It invigorated them, and we could see how much they loved the place and the children. We knew that Mount Hope was going to need seasoned, faithful, and wise leaders and felt the leading of the Lord to ask them if they would consider moving to West Kalimantan to take over the operational leadership of the campus. They were thrilled to be asked as they had felt that their time serving at the bible college was ending, and this was a great fit for them. They happily accepted and we entrusted them with this project, knowing they would do an incredible job leading it.

Abraham and Melanie had been at Mount Hope for about a year when one day, Abraham took a trip up the river to a place he had heard about called Sungkung. Much of Kalimantan is rainforest which is so dense there are no roads. However, many rivers wind through the jungle, and boat travel is the only way to access the remote settlements in the interior. To get to Sungkung, Abraham travelled a good seven or eight hours by motorised canoe, finally arriving at the habitation, which he discovered to be very primitive, poverty-stricken, and without a school. Abraham introduced himself to the area chief and asked if he could speak to the parents about Mount Hope school. The response was overwhelming as many parents came to talk to him, interested to find out more and wondering if it would be an option for their children.

Over several subsequent visits, Abraham built trust with the Sungkung community, and we began to see parents bring their small children to be schooled by us. This was such a massive vote of confidence for our staff. That these families would entrust us enough to send their young ones so far away to be educated, knowing they would not see their kids for weeks or often months, was a huge privilege and a big responsibility at the same time.

Many of these families were so poor that they could not afford to send for their children, nor visit them, even when holidays came. As much as we would have liked, we knew we couldn't contribute to sending the children back home for every holiday either. We were already at budget with the operating costs of the school, and there were just too many of them from that village to make it a viable option.

For many of our pupils from Sungkung the school became their home. They lived at Mount Hope for much of the year, patiently waiting for the day when their parents could send enough money for them to go back to their family. For some this may have only been once or twice a year. Although at times they missed their parents, the children often said they preferred to stay at Mount Hope than go home, and we knew this was because of the poverty in the village. Most of them looked on Abraham and Melanie as their surrogate parents, who loved the children as if they were their own.

◆ ◆ ◆

Today, Mount Hope is a place of much laughter and noise, but also routine and care. All five hundred students are taught the bible among other subjects and yet, interestingly, we have Muslim children who attend our school. We are non-apologetic about being a Christian school, but still their parents bring their children because of the standard of education we offer.

All of the hundred and fifty live-in children attend early morning prayer. In Indonesia the day starts early anyway as it's warm and bright, so getting up to pray at 5.30 a.m. is not a big adjustment for them. We begin by singing praise and worship songs, with the kids joining in enthusiastically. The children then divide into groups with a staff member who leads them through prayer and bible reading appropriate to their ages.

Breakfast is served straight after prayer—this is usually a rice dish with vegetables, or noodles, or some type of porridge. As 7 a.m. nears, the school swells with the arrival of three hundred and fifty local students, all in uniform and ready for classes. Once the 'day students' leave, we serve another hot meal, and the afternoon is then filled with siesta, chores, free time, and sports. After dinner we have devotions, once again broken up into age groups. Even the youngest children are encouraged to read scriptures out loud, even if it is just a couple of words or a sentence.

The children at Mount Hope are content—they have nutritious, well-balanced meals, a bed to sleep on with clean sheets in a peaceful dormitory, and people who love and care for them. The school runs on a good routine, which provides structure and certainty to their lives. I have not known of many behavioural problems amongst the kids, and even the teenagers are pleasant, content, and very grateful for the opportunity for a good education. Most days, our classes are filled with young and eager students who want to learn and do well.

◆ ◆ ◆

One day, about five years after the school commenced, Carol and I were looking out over the school complex. We had just arrived from Java and had brought a load of used clothes with us which people from around Java had donated for the children at Mount Hope. These donations always cause much excitement for the kids as they carefully pick through the items, eager for something new to wear.

As we sat there, we could see the children coming in and out of their rooms, trying on various clothing items. A group of little girls were having so much fun, giggling as they modelled their outfits to each other. They were so delighted to receive these gifts of used clothes that we felt joyful just watching them. That day, Tanti, one of the three siblings from the jungle, was among them, dancing around, joy lighting up her face. It was very special to see them all dressed up looking so proud of themselves, especially at the Sunday service when many of them ran to give us hugs, affectionately calling us *Oma* and *Opa*[7]. I thought back to the time when our own children had left home and Carol and I had a desire to foster kids. Looking around at the sea of young faces now, I knew that God had fulfilled that longing in an extraordinary way.

Joli, Tanti and Yogi lived at Mount Hope until they finished their schooling about ten years after they first arrived. We all celebrated on the day they graduated from our school to go on to further studies. They had all done very well, and as a staff, we felt so proud of them. The siblings have grown and are now married with children of their own. All three still live close to Mount Hope, and it is a blessing to see them now bring *their* children to attend our school.

---

7 Grandmother and Grandfather

CHAPTER NINETEEN

Kartika was another student whose story touched our hearts. One of our staff members was visiting his family in a village a couple of hours away when he saw a young girl hanging back from the rest of the children who were happily playing tag together. He noticed something different about the way she was moving, and soon realised that the reason Kartika was not interacting with the others was because her feet were facing backwards and the wrong way up. She had been born with clubfeet, and although she could walk and even run a little, it was only ever for short distances, and her walk was more of a limp and her run a hobble.

Her condition was cause for much distress as the other children relentlessly picked on her and teased her for being different. Even her parents had accepted that this was their daughter's lot and had stopped protecting her from the insults. As a result, Kartika withdrew further and further into herself and had no self-confidence.

Our staff member felt that her quality of life would be better at Mount Hope as the children were taught to love one another as Christ loves and accepts us. Her parents had heard of the school, and agreed that it would be a better option for her.

Moving into the dormitory was a big step for the nine-year-old. Kartika had come from a small village which was only accessible by foot or motorbike. She was painfully shy and would not engage at all at first. She could not look people in the eye but would hang her head and whisper so quietly it was as if she just wanted to disappear. Our hearts broke for this young girl who was filled with shame and fear—the result of voices who had chosen to ridicule her rather than speak life over her.

The weeks turned into months, and slowly but surely, as our staff loved on her, Kartika began to open her heart and learn to trust. She realised that in this new environment she was accepted just as she was by our staff, teachers, and the children. For the first time in many years, she found friends who loved her. She was content and happy and grew in confidence. Kartika loved her schoolwork and absorbed knowledge quickly, proving to be an intelligent young girl.

Wondering what could be done to further help her, our staff began to research available medical procedures that would give her a better future. Visits to local doctors proved futile—in the medical world she was seen as too old for clubfoot reversal surgery to be effective.

One of our ministry partners, Craig Pilcher, a builder from New Zealand, was enroute to Indonesia, visiting a friend who was a medical doctor in Kuching, Malaysia. When he talked about Kartika's predicament the doctor agreed to have a look to see if he could do anything. This was a breakthrough as other medical practitioners had declined because of her age, so Craig was hopeful. However, persuading Kartika's parents was not an easy task. For a couple who were from a small and quite remote village to consider travelling to another *country* to see a doctor who *may* be able to help their daughter was a huge step both practically and mentally. After many discussions and much encouragement from our staff, they finally consented, and our team got to work organising passports.

Once in Malaysia, Craig's associate was able to refer Kartika's case on to a more specialised doctor. This miraculously led to a treatment plan which was decided on by a whole team of specialists. The therapy was going to take several months of ongoing manipulation of the foot, and the treatment was going to cost twenty-five thousand dollars. The high cost of the treatment and the idea of living in Malaysia was just too much for Kartika's parents to comprehend. Once again, our staff team took the time to explain why we believed this was the right thing to do, assuring them that we would pray, and that God would provide through His people. They could not see how this could happen, but to their credit, put their trust in our team, and armed with the hope that this treatment could mean a better life for Kartika, they gave the go-ahead.

As Craig and our staff team began to spread the word, people from different parts of the world contributed to Kartika's treatment, and before long the money had come in and the treatment on her foot commenced. Kartika and her mother stayed in Malaysia for almost six months, where they were looked after by a gracious Christian family. The hospital staff were exemplary, taking all their needs into consideration, even the transport to and from appointments.

After six months of arduous treatment, Kartika's feet were facing forward and the right side up. She had patiently endured months of pain and surgery, and was rewarded with a successful outcome. When she arrived back at Mount Hope, not only was she excited to be home but judging by the peals of laughter and joy from the other children, they were happy to see her, especially now she was walking so much easier.

Kartika's physical healing was so obvious, but so was the healing of her emotions. Her self-confidence grew in leaps and bounds over this time. No longer was she the shy, retiring girl who could not look us in the eye—she was now a young lady who could ride a bike, and enjoyed being the star performer in dance and drama.

Two years after she arrived at Mount Hope, Kartika walked back into her parents' village for the first time since she had left. Like moths to a light the villagers gathered around her to look at her feet and to hear the story. They could not believe how a group of strangers could go to all that trouble to help her. The many acts of kindness that had contributed to Kartika's healing spoke volumes to the small community of God's love. They couldn't understand it, but they knew it must be a good God that would cause this to happen.

In subsequent months we heard how Kartika's story was acknowledged as a success in the medical world and was used as a case study in a medical journal. Whether God heals through a miracle of instant healing or by using the hands of a team of talented medics, He *still* gets the glory!

❖ ❖ ❖

As time went on, Carol and I began dividing our time between Mount Hope in Kalimantan, and the bible college in Java. We would travel to Mount Hope every four months to check on the progress and encourage our staff there. The rest of the time, we were in Tawangmangu, where I was teaching several subjects.

There were still deep hostilities between the Dayaks and the Madurese peoples, and we could sense a growing undercurrent of discord. We also heard that the local Dayak people had started to import weapons from their counterparts in Malaysia and were transporting them over the Malay-Indonesian border.

Because Mount Hope was so close to the border, we often went to Malaysia for supplies or to pick up overseas guests from the airport. Seemingly overnight, the border controls, which consisted of a small shack with a couple of guards, expanded into imposing-looking buildings with uniformed staff and a substantial military presence. At one point, when we were driving close to the border, we were stopped by the Indonesian military to check if we had weapons.

Sadly, everything came to a head and war broke out between the tribes. Although this didn't affect us as it was some distance from Mount Hope, we received regular updates from church planters who were closer to the uprising. Reports were coming of many deaths, and one of our church planters had the horrific experience of seeing a truck drive by with the decapitated heads of the Dayak's enemies. Their custom was to take the severed heads to their villages where they would put them on poles to keep evil spirits away. It was not a pleasant time, and we continually prayed that God's peace would permeate the area and cause the hostilities to cease. Eventually the fighting did end, and we were thankful that no one we knew was hurt.

◆ ◆ ◆

Even amidst the unrest, the Lord was blessing the work at Mount Hope—so much so, that seven years after receiving my vision from the Lord, we had reached capacity. Since the start of the project, the building work had never stopped, due to the constant need to take in more children. We had built a kindergarten, primary school, junior high school and dormitories. With one hundred and sixty live-in children, the dorms were packed, and with the increase in students came an increase in staff, who also needed housing. By now we had come to the boundary line near the staff quarters and needed more land to build additional accommodation.

Craig Pilcher, the builder who made regular visits to help with the building projects, suggested we buy a small section of the two-and-a-half-hectare property adjacent to Mount Hope. He calculated that an additional fifteen metres would be enough for a good-sized home for our new staff. He and our on-site builder, Tony, decided to approach the landowner to see the land and negotiate a price.

Unbeknown to us, the landowner had already been offered $350,000 for the full section from a wealthy businessman, but had declined the offer! When our staff told him we wanted to buy approximately fifteen metres of the land, he said, "Why don't you just buy the lot?" He told us that if we bought the whole section from him, he would sell it to us for $35,000!

We couldn't understand why he would sell it to us so cheaply, when he could have made much more money had he taken the businessman's offer. Eventually the landowner explained that he had seen the results of what we were doing and noticed that we were trying to help the local people, and he wanted to support us. We were touched to hear this and so moved by the man's generosity. Wasting no time, Craig and Tony signed the papers to buy the additional property.

God has provided so abundantly for every stage of the Mount Hope project. Today, Mount Hope sits on twenty-five hectares of beautiful property with thirteen main buildings, and a new primary school building currently being constructed. On the property is also a small pig farm, a fish farm, and a pepper farm, enabling us to be more self-sufficient. The homegrown meat and fish are for the children and staff, while excess produce is sold at the markets, providing extra income for the school. The fishpond has aquaponic plants growing on top of the water, offering beautiful green vegetables for the school children and staff. I had seen a picture of green plants growing on the fishponds in the vision God gave me and yet I didn't even know what aquaponics was at the time. God knows so much more than I do, but I am so thankful that as we follow His leading, we get to learn new things along the way!

◆ ◆ ◆

As the lives of the community surrounding Mount Hope became intertwined with us through our school, we were able to bless the community in other ways. Around this time, some of our Mount Hope staff became aware of elderly people in the local village who were being neglected. Walking back from the market, they noticed aged people sitting outside their homes, asleep in the shade. On closer investigation our staff learned that their families were out all day working in the rice fields and were unable to look after the grandparents, many who were very frail or even sick.

In that town, there are no retirement villages or old people's homes. It is customary for each family to look after their elderly family members. As such, a traditional family is not just 'nuclear' but consists of extended families living together.

Recognising this as an opportunity to help, our staff met some of these families and offered to check in on their elderly relatives during the day when possible. The families were very thankful, but as our team began dropping in on these residents, they found that many were ill or physically unable to feed themselves. Lying around hungry all day, they had to wait until the rest of the family came home to get a meal or other care. Within a couple of weeks, it became apparent that this was a pressing need, so our team approached the local council and communicated that we wanted to help these older people. We suggested that if the government could help financially, we could assist with feeding and caring for the elderly in our village. The idea was favourable to the council, who promptly sent us some money to get this initiative going.

With the funds from the government, we bought ten piglets which we fed and cared for, then once they were grown, a few of the pigs were sold to buy enough food for the elderly. The rest were kept for reproduction to fund ongoing feeding programmes. Our staff cooked meals and delivered them to the ones who needed them most. As they brought meals, the elderly people started to trust our staff, who often had opportunities to pray for them and share the good news during their visits.

The families of these elderly people were so grateful for our help with their parents, and this layer of care from our staff, on top of the great name Mount Hope had already, spoke volumes to the surrounding neighbourhood. This initiative continued for thirteen years, until all the people that we knew were in need had passed away. By this point, the standard of living in the area had improved remarkably and families were able to better look after their elderly.

As a leader, I could not have been prouder of the initiative that our staff took with this. They could have been restricted to the task of running the kindergarten and school which is a busy and time-consuming job in itself, but their eyes had been open as they walked slowly through the community. They allowed the Lord to lead them to places where He wanted to show His kindness. We have found that there are always ways to help, and if we allow God to lead, He uses us in ways we never would have thought of. Often it starts in the most practical and small ways, but as we are obedient, He entrusts us with more. I believe this is what living faith looks like.

◆ ◆ ◆

Over the years, the Indonesian government began to invest in the island, and the standard of living in the Balaikarangan area improved dramatically—to the point where we can now charge school fees for families who can pay. This allows us to keep taking in the poorer children and orphans, and look after them for free. We have seen such a turnaround in Kalimantan, and as a result, there is a declining number of those who need sponsorship.

Other schools have also been built, even in remote locations, which solves the education problem for many in the poorest parts. However, even with the availability of other schools, Mount Hope has become the sought-after option, and we have gained an excellent reputation. Several years ago, we received an award for being the best school in the region, and we have a long wait list of families wanting to enrol their children.

It is a delight to know that through Mount Hope, many hundreds of children have accepted Jesus Christ as their Lord and Saviour. Our team have had the privilege of discipling them and watching them grow in their faith as they go through the school. It has also been a joy to have some of these students return to us years later to be employed as staff and teachers. We know the spiritual landscape of Kalimantan has changed due to the hundreds of students who have found hope in Christ and are now living out their future in Him.

As the spiritual landscape has transformed, so has the physical landscape of Balaikarangan and the wider region. On a visit after a number of years, our daughter Marissa commented that what once was an insignificant, dirty, neglected town with a couple of lifeless shops had become a thriving municipality with a bustling market. There were now *many* shops and eating places lining the main street, and a feeling of life as villagers go about their days with purpose. I was grateful that we had changed the name of the hill. As we declared Mount Hope would bring a future and a hope to the children in our school, the wider community was also being impacted by the Lord's goodness.

CHAPTER TWENTY

Back in Java, the Asian Financial Crisis was hitting hard. In the first six months of the crisis, the value of the Indonesian rupiah dropped by eighty per cent, causing prices of essential everyday items to soar, and we watched as many plunged into poverty. Every day the newspapers featured stories of big businesses going bankrupt and thousands losing their jobs. Unemployment in the nation had hit a critical point. Growing tension and anger towards the Indonesian government led to mobs of unemployed young men, primarily Javanese, seeking an outlet for their frustration and anger. Sadly, it was the Chinese Indonesian people who became their target.

We felt the sting of injustice as our Chinese friends became fearful that the Javanese, who were normally gentle, peaceful people, would rob their homes, destroy their vehicles, or harm their children. This was happening to other Chinese around them, predominantly because they were seen to be financially successful. Also, many were perceived to be Christians. This presumption came about when years earlier, the Indonesian government brought in 'National Identity Cards' for all citizens, whereby every person had to declare their religious affiliation. Many of the Chinese ticked the 'Christian' category even though they may not have been a practising Christian. The fact that they chose Christianity over Islam was further cause for friction.

Widespread rioting peaked in May 1998 leading to President Suharto stepping down from office due to public pressure. Political instability on top of everything else caused fear to be rampant throughout the country. Many Chinese tried to escape to Singapore and further abroad, and airports filled with queues of panicking people. Even our small town of Tawangmangu, high up on the mountainside, was not immune from the feeling of insecurity and unrest. College was out for the semester, so we only had a handful of students plus our staff on-site. We were still gathering as usual for prayer meetings; however, not wanting to attract the attention of possible rioters, we turned off all the lights and had our evening prayer meetings by candlelight.

We could see how much the economic situation was affecting people all around us. There was a conspicuous rise in street beggars, especially in the cities. When we stopped at traffic lights in Solo, they swarmed around us, thrusting their hands into the tiniest opening of the car window, hoping to receive something. We would constantly hand out cash. Often it wasn't much money, but knowing it only took a few rupiahs to keep someone from starving, we gave what we could.

My heart broke for the older men who could no longer find work and had lost dignity and respect. I felt compassion for the mother sitting outside the bank begging with a sick baby in her arms and her skinny toddler playing on the dirty sidewalk, and we wished we had more to give to the many children who peered into our car, their brown eyes filled with hope and their hands outstretched. When we had no notes left on us, we would give coins, food, anything.

Lack was all around, and I knew we needed to do something more. We talked about it with our staff and decided to ask our local mayor which villages were the most impoverished. Then we resolved to fast a day every fortnight and use our food money for that day to buy staples for them. Because there were quite a few of us, we were able to donate a fair amount of food to the villagers. It was such a joyful experience to load up the truck with sacks of rice, oil, tea and other food and, along with our mayor, distribute it to the ones who needed it most.

Our local city of Solo became an epicentre for the revolt. Mobs looted local businesses, bringing everything out onto the streets to set it alight in a big bonfire. Our local police warned us to be careful and not to travel down the mountain to the city. We were to stay put for several weeks until all the unrest died down.

Meanwhile, a guest from New Zealand who was teaching at the college felt he needed to return home due to the political situation. He was getting more nervous as the days went by and flights out of Indonesia became scarce. Carol rang the New Zealand embassy in Jakarta, and thankfully they were able to obtain passage for him out of the country. We informed our local police that our guest needed to get to Solo—our nearest airport—in order to leave. As the situation was volatile, and they were concerned for our safety, the police arranged for an army officer to accompany my guest and me to the airport. Although we took all the back routes to the airport and didn't go through the city, I was dismayed to see such disorder. Even on the backstreets, there were empty business buildings with broken windows covered in graffiti, and in the distance, we could see pillars of smoke from smouldering bonfires.

When we were finally able to go into the city, Carol and I were shocked by the devastation. What was a bustling, flourishing centre had been decimated in a matter of weeks. The bonfires had ravaged the streets, leaving them scorched and full of holes. Many prominent buildings, mostly Chinese-owned banks and shops, were left in ruins. To see our city so severely affected was painful, and we felt deep grief as we wondered how long it would take to rebuild. It was a relief when the riots died down, but over the next few years, there was an underlying current of unrest and dissatisfaction in the nation, with ongoing pockets of flare-ups.

◆ ◆ ◆

It took a long time for things to settle down. Almost a year later, we were in Solo with our kids who were on holiday from New Zealand. After spending some time shopping, we decided to get some lunch before we left the city. There was a nice restaurant on the city's outskirts where we stopped, found a large table by the window, and ordered our food. The soup promptly arrived at our table, steaming hot and smelling tasty, and Marissa and Ronn, who had craved Indonesian food while overseas, were eager to tuck in.

We had just prayed a blessing over the meal when we heard a commotion outside. Surprised, we looked up to see an angry mob of men moving swiftly towards the restaurant. They were yelling as they punched the air with their fists in defiance. Alarm bells went off in my head, and my 'fight or flight' instinct kicked in. Suddenly, glass shattered as rocks flew through the windows on the far side of the restaurant. I quickly jumped up to move my family, who were stunned as they watched cars being upturned in the car park. Several men rushed into the restaurant, and one came up to me and yelled for us to get out quickly—this was a Chinese-owned restaurant, and they were going to set it alight. I hastily ushered the family out, jostling angry men as we made our way to the car, praying it was still intact.

Thankfully, our vehicle was still upright, and we quickly got in and sped away from the chaos, turning our eyes back to see what was unfolding. We were all shaken, and as the adrenalin and emotions wore off, we settled in to talk about it on the way home. We knew God had protected us. All six of us were physically unharmed and the mob had not touched our car, for which we were grateful. Emotionally, we were shaken and tense, but I knew that would heal. We prayed for the restaurant owners, no doubt now without a business for a while, and asked for God's protection over them. We learned later that the restaurant was closed for several weeks and had sustained damage, but the building was still intact and, thankfully, the owners unharmed. Even so, the oppression towards minority groups in Indonesia was still not over.

Several weeks later we received an urgent phone call from our local police, warning us to quickly hide our vehicles. An extremist Muslim faction was on their way up the mountain in a convoy of trucks carrying rebels. Their target was our bible college. Having already burnt shops in the town south of us, only twenty minutes away, we didn't have much time, but at least if we hid our vehicles in the village, we would have the chance to get away if the worst eventuated.

All our students were in class, and there wasn't enough time to get the word around to evacuate them. Carol and I prayed quickly, and as we did, two things came to mind which led me to believe God would protect us. The first was Psalm 41:1-2:

> *Blessed is the one who considers the poor! In the day of trouble, the Lord delivers him; the Lord protects him and keeps him alive; he is called blessed in the land; you do not give him up to the will of his enemies.*

I gained confidence from this scripture. When we care for the poor and needy, as we had just done for the villagers, God would not give us up 'to the will of our enemies'.

The second impression I got was that God had prepared me for this moment. A month prior, I had been invited to speak in a large church which had recently experienced a bombing. The church was the latest target in a succession of church bombings by extremist Muslims. On arrival at the church, the pastor asked me if I'd heard about the bombs, to which I responded affirmatively. He proceeded to lead me into the church auditorium and showed me where the terrorists had planted three bombs. Two smaller bombs were hidden on either side of the hall, and one big one in the centre underneath the floor.

The Christians had been celebrating their annual Christmas programme, and the church, which seated about eight hundred people, was packed. Suddenly, in the middle of the service, the two smaller bombs detonated, causing explosions on either side of the building. Chaos ensued as over eight hundred screaming people panicked and fled the building, but amazingly no one had been hurt!

A Christian policeman happened to be sitting right beside one of the bombs that went off. He sat stunned as he checked himself over. His nice suit jacket and trousers were ripped to shreds from the shrapnel, but his body was untouched! He did not have a single scratch from the bomb! His testimony to his superior at work the following day was that Jesus protects His own.

Interestingly, the middle bomb never exploded and was later removed by the bomb squad. They deduced that there was a strategy for the side bombs to detonate first, forcing everyone to run to the middle of the church, which was when the big one—big enough to kill everyone—would go off. Praise the Lord, God had suppressed that giant bomb from detonating! Seeing the remains of the fragments on the walls and the ceilings, it had to be a miracle that no one was hurt. It was indeed a testimony of God's incredible protection.

Now, back at the bible college, I knew the same God who protected those church members could also protect us. Climbing the stairs to my office, I waited and prayed, "Lord, You are our refuge and strength, a very present help in time of trouble."

Fifteen minutes lapsed. My ears were pricked for the sounds of traffic. "Thank you that You will not give us up to the will of our enemies …"

Twenty minutes passed, and nothing happened.

They would have been here by now, I thought.

Thirty minutes—nothing.

The hour ticked into the next and then the next, and still nothing.

No attack.

No unwanted visitors.

No disruption to the normal.

Our students who had been made aware of the threats were on the alert but continued their day as usual. Many of the young people in the area began to gather at our gates. They had heard that our school was the target and felt protective of us. Even though many of them were Muslims, they had seen what we had done to help with the food donations and, just like us, they wanted peace in their town.

As evening descended, these local youths took turns alongside our students and staff to guard our gates and keep watch through the night. For a whole week, we had people from the local community coming alongside to stand guard. We were so blessed by this show of solidarity amongst our neighbours and local villagers, and made sure we looked after them with food and hot drinks to keep them going through the night.

Several days later, a government representative visited us to give an update. I asked him why the extremist group never made it to the school. He started to describe how the army had set up a barricade in the road coming up to Tawangmangu. At this point, his voice trailed off and he looked confused. He didn't seem to know why the terrorists had not made it, but we knew! God had sent His angels just as He promised.

For he will command his angels concerning you
to guard you in all your ways.

Psalm 91:11

Although we had seen God's protection over us, the stress of the event had traumatised Carol. For weeks after this, whenever she was sitting at her desk, which faced the road, the sounds of trucks going by would cause her to panic. Knowing she had to overcome this, my brave wife printed out portions of Psalm 91 and pasted them to the top of her laptop so they were always in front of her. When the feelings of panic started to rise, she read the verses out loud to remind herself of God's protection, and as she did this, her faith was strengthened. Little by little, as she kept declaring scripture over her emotions, fear began to dissipate until eventually it completely disappeared, and thankfully, she was free from the trauma.

CHAPTER TWENTY-ONE

While the uprisings were happening in Java, over in Ambon, an extremist Muslim faction was involved in what became known as 'Holy Wars'. They were actively advertising for people to join the revolution to fight against the Christians.

Sitting in the car outside the bank in Solo one day, Carol saw a poster calling for recruits to join the fight over in Ambon. The strategy of the extremist group was to turn the Maluku Islands, a predominantly Christian area, into a Muslim stronghold. The movement was gathering momentum as they recruited far and wide, even pulling people from Pakistan and the Middle East.

Face-offs between nominal Christians and Muslims in Ambon had been going on for several months. They were killing each other in the streets, and it was a terrible time for those Ambonese who did not want to get involved but were inadvertently caught up and had to fight to defend themselves. As a result, many were leaving town to hide in the mountains. Those who could leave the island fled to other parts of Indonesia. Even my aged parents, who lived in the middle of the city of Ambon, had to flee from their house. With all the fighting and chaos, many children became separated from their parents and took to hiding in empty homes or in the forests.

One Sunday when I was ministering in East Java, the pastor of the church challenged his people to do something to help the Ambonese kids, many of whom had been orphaned due to the fighting. The Muslims were actively taking these children and putting them into Muslim boarding schools, and he wanted his church to get involved. This news caught me off guard. I didn't know this was happening to the Ambonese children, and I felt a burden in my heart about this. I knew that with this knowledge, I was now responsible to do something.

The following Sunday morning, back at the bible college, I challenged our students and staff to take up an offering for the Ambonese children. We had heard that many kids were left hiding in churches or empty halls in Ambon while their parents fought and knew that if we didn't get to them quickly, they would end up in Muslim schools. Not wanting this to happen, we started to plan how to get the children out of Ambon and bring them to safety. The offering that day was the most significant offering we had ever taken up to that point. Our students and staff had so much compassion and gave generously, even giving their rings and jewellery, sacrificing what they had for these children.

Following the offering we sent one of our staff members to find out more about the situation. Nocke was originally from Ambon and had many contacts there who could protect him and inform him about the areas to avoid. On his arrival he discovered some older ladies who were looking after the children in empty halls and churches while they waited for parents to come back for the kids. It was such a volatile and unsafe place for them, and it was only a matter of time before they were discovered by the extremists. Nocke spoke with those looking after the children and offered to help bring them to Java, where they would be safe. He was known and trusted in Ambon, and the guardians wanted him to get the children out as quickly as possible.

A few days later Nocke told us that he was on his way back to Java, bringing eighty children with him. I wondered how he would handle that many kids on his own, but we immediately started looking for a place that could become their new home. We did not know how long we would have these children or what the next step would be, but we knew they were in danger and that we could provide safety in Tawangmangu.

Carol and a couple of our staff wasted no time finding a large home down the road from us. It was perfect, as it had seven huge bedrooms plus several other large living spaces. The only drawback was that there was no furniture.

The offering money had been used to purchase tickets for the three-day journey on a ship plus bus trips to bring the children to Java. There was no money left to buy the necessary furniture and household items we needed to create a new home for the children—beds, mattresses, sheets, towels, kitchenware and toiletries, for a start. Then there was the question of how many personal items such as clothes and toys, the children would have with them—I guessed it would be minimal.

Praise the Lord that by now we had internet access, so Carol sent out an urgent email to our supporters asking for help. She explained the predicament of these children and outlined the list of supplies we needed. The response from that email was overwhelming. People's hearts were moved with compassion for the plight of these kids, and the donations were so generous that we were able to buy all the immediate needs, and even had enough to buy a minibus to transport the children! All this happened within a few days, and we were so thankful for people who could give generously and promptly.

◆ ◆ ◆

The week sped by quickly as our team gathered furniture and household items, cleaned the house, made the beds, and set up the kitchen so it was ready to go. The house was simple but clean and tidy. The bedrooms had several giant beds which would sleep four or five small children, and there were mattresses arranged all over the floor of the bedrooms and into the extensive living areas. We were ready! All we had to do was wait to welcome these children whom we had not yet met but already loved.

It was evening when Nocke and the kids finally arrived. They ranged from six to fifteen years of age and many of them had just become orphans, while others didn't know where their parents were or even if they were still alive. They descended from the buses, tired from three days of travel and emotionally exhausted from the previous few weeks, and as I looked at their faces marred with fear, sorrow, and uncertainty, I was overwhelmed with compassion for them. Judging from the expression on my wife and our team's faces, they felt the same. We showed the children around their new home and helped them unpack. They had few personal belongings, so it didn't take long.

Just as they were settling in we heard blasts of gunfire in the distance. As residents, we were aware that the local army regiment was carrying out training exercises in the nearby forest, so this did not catch us off guard. To the kids, however, the gunfire triggered fresh memories, and their reaction was an immediate uproar. The younger ones started screaming and crying, whilst the older ones became visibly tense and edgy. Some even asked for weapons.

We were sorry that the first night had started so traumatically but within minutes, our staff were reassuring the children, cradling the little ones on laps, pulling the older ones in with big hugs and soothing voices, offering closeness and protection to all.

After this unfortunate start, the children slowly became accustomed to their new lives. We quickly introduced a routine with classes at the local school, meals, playtime, and bedtime, and they responded positively to their new environment, but it was the love of the staff members who cared for them that had the most significant impact and caused their hearts to heal.

It was soon clear that Nocke and his wife had fallen in love with the kids, and the children loved them back. Their own children had grown up and left home, and now they cared for these orphans like their own. They were the obvious choice to become permanent house parents, and we were so glad when they readily accepted our request. Not surprisingly, on any given day, we would find the bible college staff also at the house. They would drop in for quick visits, eager to check on how the children were doing, bringing an abundance of hugs, and giving out oranges and snacks as a treat. The home was becoming a centre of love, care and joy, a tangible symbol of God's love in action, which spoke volumes to our surrounding community.

In Ambon the 'holy wars' were continuing to rage and Nocke became aware of more children needing to be rescued. On receiving further requests from his contacts, asking if we could take in more children, Nocke once again made the trip to Ambon. This time he returned with sixty children, bringing the number of kids in our care to one hundred and forty! We rented another house, and other Christians in the area also opened their homes to the children. Incredibly, Carol never had to send out a request for more support—people far and near were moved by the plight of these kids and ensured that the children never lacked for anything.

Most of the children ended up staying with us for about three years. During this time we taught them the Word of God and showed them how to pray. Many of them had so much hatred in their lives after what they had gone through. It soon came out in the way they spoke about, and interacted with, others at school, especially Muslims. It was difficult for us to see such strong feelings in children so young, but as our team led them to Jesus and taught them of His love for them, they began to forgive, let go of the hate, and walk freely in forgiveness and peace. For some, the transformation was particularly noticeable. Instead of being aggressive and fractious, the children were happy, content and they laughed more which was beautiful to see.

It was always a jubilant occasion when those whose parents were still alive were reconnected with their families. Many surviving parents who had escaped from Ambon and moved to other islands, eventually took their children back to start a new life together. Gradually the number of residents at the children's home dwindled, but the orphans remained. By now they had bonded with Nocke and his wife and were flourishing.

Years later, some of the children we cared for over that time returned to attend our bible college. What a joy it was to see how they had grown, and to be part of their lives again! One of the boys Nocke rescued from Ambon eventually came on staff and is now part of our team in Mount Hope. We are so thankful that we were able to step in and help these children. God provided so beautifully in every aspect of their lives, and we rejoice that they have been able to move forward as healed, whole and loving human beings.

❖ ❖ ❖

In the years since taking over the leadership of the bible college, we had witnessed many hundreds of miracles of God's transforming power and healing, as well as provision in the lives of our students. We were offering a four-year degree course in theology and our staff rejoiced each year as we graduated and commissioned our students, knowing that He who began a good work would bring it to completion. We also invested into their ongoing lives through regular prayer and by keeping in touch with many of them, even years after they had graduated from college.

There is no denying the testimony of a changed life and in my view, this is the greatest miracle ever. We saw hardened ex-convicts become gracious, forgiving ministers; broken and rejected young ones who had been kicked out of their homes and communities since receiving Christ become whole, on-fire missionaries spreading the love of God wherever they went; we watched uneducated and simple village teenagers become switched on by the power of God's Word and on graduating from our college, take positions of influence in the government. It was the story of the potter and the clay over and over again, and we had front-row seats witnessing the Father's love in action, moulding and creating new vessels fit for His use.

◆ ◆ ◆

By now, all four of our children were completing their various educational journeys in New Zealand, and we wondered if there was some way for us to buy a family home for whenever we visited. Carol and I had never owned our own home—there didn't seem to be much point, as we already had places to live both at the bible college and Mount Hope. The only time we ever had to think about accommodation was when we visited our children in New Zealand. Most of the time we would rent a house, however this wasn't always an easy option as leases were normally for a year, and we only ever needed to stay for a few months at the most.

Although Carol never said anything, she enjoyed looking at houses for sale whenever we walked past a real estate agent's window in New Zealand. I knew that in her heart she would love a home of our own.

One day, a pastor in New Zealand who had supported our work for many years, asked, "Have you ever considered buying a house to return to one day?" His question seemed to come out of the blue, yet I had no hesitation when I told him yes, but we didn't know how. I had no idea of the cost of land in New Zealand, but I knew the New Zealand dollar was much stronger than the Indonesian rupiah and guessed that this could be an expensive exercise.

I was unprepared for my friend Rob's next statement. "We will try and make it happen for you," he simply said.

I did not know how Rob would do this, but I recognised that this was a 'God-moment'—a moment when faith speaks, and vision is captured. This man had faith for such a venture and a seed was planted in both Carol's heart and mine.

Carol was excited about the prospect of us owning a home for the first time in our married lives. She loved looking at magazines of beautiful houses and had always tried her best to make our homes look stylish and comfortable. Although we wouldn't spend much time in this house, I could see Carol was already dreaming about how nice it would be to stay in our own property whenever we were in New Zealand.

Several months passed and one day during a phone call, Rob told us he had found a good plot to build on and that we needed to put down a deposit to secure the land. We did not have enough savings at the time, but remembered that our mission organisation had a retirement fund set up for us. After making some enquiries, we happily were able to access the funds. This gave half the amount we needed for the deposit, and without us even asking, kind family members who knew we wanted a home of our own gave generously to help us buy the land.

The site Rob had found was on a hill in Wellington which gave us a lovely outlook over the surrounding neighbourhood and a glimpse of the ocean. With all our savings now spent on the procurement of the land, we had no funds left for the build. With clever financial management, however, and some further funding, Rob was able to get the ball rolling and before long a beautiful house had been built, without us having to lift a finger! It was an incredible feeling to be homeowners, and Carol was overjoyed, even though we were seven thousand kilometres away.

By now Ronn and Marissa were married, and Jeffrey was flatting in Wellington, so it was our daughter Sheryl who lived in the house, along with friends who shared the rent with her. The house became our family's hub where they would gather for Christmas and birthdays to celebrate with their spouses and small families. Although Carol and I were not able to be with them, as a father I was happy that our kids could enjoy the blessing of our home.

When the time came around for our next missionary 'leave', Carol and I were finally able to stay in our own home! This was a dream come true for my wife. From the moment we walked in the front door and for the next three months we enjoyed every minute of being there. God had poured so much rich blessing on our lives, and we revelled in it!

Those three months were the only time we stayed in that home. Over the years that followed our kids married and moved into their own houses, and we were able to rent the house out to others. Our plan was that whenever we visited New Zealand, we would stay with our children's families so we could make the most of every minute we had with them and the grandkids.

A year after returning to Indonesia, we heard again from Rob that the housing market was so favourable in New Zealand that the equity in the house was now enough to buy *another* property. We could not believe it! The second home transaction was as easy and painless as the first, and before we knew it, we had gone from having no home of our own to owning two rental properties in a matter of a few years!

Many years later, on the advice of financially astute friends, we eventually sold both houses and made good profit which then was deposited into a high yield investment fund. Just like the mustard seed in the parable Jesus told, which grows into a tree, giving food and shelter for the birds, our investment also keeps on giving. In recent years we have been able to give substantial amounts from this fund back into missions, and this has given us such joy!

What started off as a blessing for Carol and me, has become a blessing for many more people. We have learned that as we run in our lane and stay faithful to what the Lord has asked us to do, He brings others alongside to partner with us in ways that we never would have thought of. We did not have the giftings or business savvy that our friend Rob has, and he cannot do what we are doing, but God caused our paths to collide in a way that has enriched both our lives and the lives of others.

CHAPTER TWENTY-TWO

It was a day that would go down in history for many in Indonesia. The clock on my desk read 5.54 a.m. when I was jolted out of prayer that Saturday morning. My office windows had started to rattle violently, and the whole house shuddered beneath me. I moved away from my windows as quickly as possible as the earthquake continued forcefully. The noise of pots and crockery clattering to the kitchen floor buried my voice as I called for Carol to get outside. We met at the door and hurried out as the ground continued to rumble. We were used to earthquakes, but this was a strong one and it seemed to go on for a long time.

"Please Lord," I prayed silently, "protect us all and keep our buildings intact." I had lived on Mount Lawu, a dormant volcano, for long enough to know what earthquakes did to concrete structures.

Once the shaking had died down and we regained our breath, we cautiously went back inside the house. Books and bric-a-brac were strewn on the floor in our lounge room, but we were relieved that there didn't seem to be any structural damage. Incredibly, our home and the rest of the college buildings were intact, and apart from shaken nerves, everyone was okay.

Sadly, this was not the case elsewhere.

Switching on the television, we discovered the earthquake measured 6.4 on the Richter scale and was centred in Bantul, a two-and-a-half-hour drive from our home. The quake had occurred close to the earth's surface, and the resulting devastation in the area was severe. In just under a minute, roads and bridges were destroyed, office buildings collapsed, and over sixty thousand homes had caved in, killing more than 3,500 people and injuring thousands more.

We felt deep grief as we watched pictures of the devastation flashing on our screen, and compassion welled up in our hearts. I knew we had to do something to help these people who had just lost their loved ones and their homes.

Several days later, Carol and I decided to visit the village along with a couple of our staff to assess the situation in Bantul to see how we could help. As we got closer to the village, we began to see groups of people scattered by the side of the road, squatting over small burners, cooking their meals. They were trying to survive in the devastation and had gathered their remaining belongings in an attempt to create order amidst the chaos. Torn mattresses and household goods covered in dust were strewn in small piles around them. With nowhere to go, they had set up home among the ruins, sleeping and eating out in the open, exposed to the hot sun and the still-settling debris.

As we got closer to the village centre, the extent of the damage became even more saddening. We had seen some footage on television, but this was worse than what we expected. Piles of broken concrete lay where houses once stood. A remnant of a building which had been the village hall stood decimated, and survivors had propped themselves up against the remaining walls. We saw families camping outside the remains of their homes, while others sheltered in whatever part of their house was still standing. Indonesian houses are built using concrete, and as this does not fare well in earthquakes, I was concerned about aftershocks.

Fortunately, by the time we arrived, the seriously injured victims had been evacuated by the army and placed in local hospitals. The remaining survivors, however, were clearly in shock. They were confused, lost and grieving, their pain so tangible that we felt it too. A couple who had moved into their newly-built home the day before the quake were now standing, traumatised, amongst the rubble. Various government and emergency aid agencies were present, helping to bring order and supply water and essentials to the survivors, but the need was overwhelming. As we spoke to people that day and tried to offer words of comfort, we knew we had to do more.

Upon arriving home, our mission organisation, having heard about the catastrophe, messaged us to ask how they could get involved. We suggested that tents would help alleviate an urgent need, so they immediately sent a donation with instructions to use it as we saw fit. Their kind contribution enabled us to buy army tents, tarpaulins, cooking utensils, and personal essentials. We also had enough money to help twenty small food vendors get set up again with foodstuffs to get their businesses up and running.

The tidy-up after the quake took quite some time. There were no big diggers or equipment to move the debris, and the survivors had to go through the rubble, pulling out reusable house materials to start rebuilding their own homes. It was a slow process, and for the most part, the clearing was done by hand.

Keen to continue helping the villagers as they rebuilt their lives, we came alongside a young couple who lived close to the area. Inge was a Christian lecturer in the nearby university, and her husband, Petrus, was a businessman. They were actively involved in the relief effort, and we eagerly supported them in whatever way we could.

Inge was concerned that the children were missing weeks of class due to the destruction of the village school. With a green light from the relevant authorities, we set up a pop-up classroom in a tent, and Inge called on some of her university students to come and run a temporary school. Not only did the children relish having something to do, it also helped keep them out of harm's way while the adults set to work rebuilding.

Noticing that several other schools in surrounding villages were also destroyed, Inge spread the word among the faculty of education at her university and was able to recruit more students and teaching staff to help. They formed other temporary classrooms—some in tents, and others in whatever buildings were structurally sound. One school was even formed in the local Mosque. The university students' efforts were invaluable, and they worked so hard keeping the makeshift classrooms going for six months until the local schools were able to open again.

Water was another concern. The main water supply to the village came via wells, several of which were damaged by the earthquake. The few that were still structurally sound were unfortunately not much use, as the water level had dropped significantly during the quake. To reach the water now required longer rope, more time, and much stronger arms. It was time-consuming and inconvenient, so with the remaining money from World Outreach, we bought electric pumps and supplies, and paid workmen to rebuild the damaged wells. In no time at all, seven village wells were back up and running. Happily, even the children were now able to draw water using the pumps.

The Bantul aid project became a focus over the ensuing weeks, and Carol and I and some of our staff regularly went to see how the rebuilds were progressing. We were always glad to see some development, but in my mind the advancements were too slow, and I began to worry about the seasonal changes coming up.

One day as Carol and I were surveying the work, I said, "It's going to be very wet and muddy soon, and these tents won't hold out the tropical rains for long." We fell quiet as our imaginations took over. The rainy season was only a couple of months away. Once it arrived, the daily downpours would turn this dusty area into a mud bath. In short, tenting in monsoon rains was not an option.

"I would love to build some simple houses to help these people," I murmured, processing my thoughts out loud. "We'd need about two hundred houses," I went on. "How about we give our monthly income as the first instalment?"

I wasn't sure how my wife would feel about the idea. We had given our months' income before, and God had always provided, but now Carol was quiet. She did not answer immediately. *Why was she hesitating?* I wondered.

"Yes, of course," she responded slowly, "but how on earth are we going to build two hundred houses in two months?"

Practical as always, she had taken a moment to think it through and was already a step ahead of me. I didn't know the answer either, but we both knew there was no time to waste. We quickly gave our money, and with Petrus' help, bought materials to start building several houses. The homes would not be flash, but the simple structures would be built out of a mixture of concrete, wood and bamboo thatch, which would keep people dry and safe, and provide a longer-term option to the tents. The residents could build them into bigger and more permanent houses as time went on.

As soon as the supplies arrived, the villagers got to work. It was encouraging to see their spirits lift and hope start to flicker in their eyes. With renewed purpose among the survivors, the pace of rebuilding started to pick up, motivating them even further. It was so wonderful to see the community coming together, as neighbours helped each other in their builds.

We knew our financial contribution would only be enough for the initial supplies to get things started, but thankfully, once word got out, other Christians and organisations began to give towards the rebuilding. Soon we had built more than two hundred simple houses for the people of Bantul, allowing the villagers to be in suitable dwellings before the rainy season. It was an absolute miracle!

Our hearts rejoiced with the survivors as they settled into their homes. We kept visiting and helping where we could until they became self-sufficient. Over time, the villagers would invite Carol and I into their homes to chat more openly with us. They told us they had been taught to believe that Christians were bad people and that it would do them no good to mix with us. However, they had observed all our efforts to help them after the quake and decided this was not the case at all. They could see that Christians were kind people who genuinely wanted to help. We were so happy to hear this and thanked the Lord that His love was felt by these people through practical acts of help.

◆ ◆ ◆

A couple of weeks later we were on a trip to Surabaya for meetings when Carol started to feel excruciating pain in one eye. She had felt a few twinges leading up to this, but it became so severe on this trip that she insisted on getting it checked.

In our giving to help build the houses for the Bantul people, we had included money which was budgeted for a specialist appointment for Carol's eyes. At the time it was not an urgent requirement, but now the situation had clearly changed.

Those who know my wife understand that she does not like drama. She is matter-of-fact, pragmatic, and never calls attention to herself, so when she says something is painful and needs immediate attention, I know to take it seriously.

The couple who was hosting us during our stay recommended an eye doctor, and although we had not made an appointment, we dropped by, hoping that he would have time to check Carol's eye. Unfortunately, he was fully booked that afternoon, but seeing that Carol was in pain, he said to come back later that evening. We told him we had an evening meeting, to which he responded that we could come after the service.

Around ten o'clock that night, we arrived at the clinic, which was adjacent to his home. Carol had been so patient, and I hoped he would be able to provide some relief quickly.

After quietly and thoroughly checking her eye, the doctor adamantly announced that he needed to operate on it immediately. Unsure whether she had heard clearly, Carol asked, "Surgery? When does this need to be done?"

"Right now!" he answered without hesitation. He explained that Carol had detached retinae in both eyes, however it was the painful eye that needed urgent attention. Without immediate surgery, he was concerned she could go blind.

To say we were surprised would be an understatement. I could see that Carol was a bit nervous, and understandably so—she was being attended to by a doctor we had never met before, telling us that without immediate attention, she could go blind. The doctor recommended using laser surgery, which we knew nothing about, other than it was an awfully expensive procedure. I felt cornered, but I knew from speaking with our hosts that this doctor was one of the best eye surgeons in the city. My wife was in so much pain, and she needed this operation.

Unable to refuse the procedure, I sat silently, mentally preparing myself to be very embarrassed, knowing we couldn't pay him as we had no money. I might have looked cool, calm, and collected on the outside, but inside I was thinking, *Oh my goodness, where will we get the money to pay for this operation?*

I started to pray nervously, not sure what else to do.

The operation was over in less than thirty minutes, and the doctor was pleased with the outcome. All had gone smoothly, and Carol's eye would heal perfectly, he said.

Heading over to the counter to 'pay', I noticed his wife, who had been assisting in the operation, whisper to her husband.

"How much do we need to pay?" I queried, apprehensively.

"No charge," he answered calmly.

Three times I asked the same question, and each time the answer was the same.

"No charge?" I repeated.

Seeing my bewilderment, the couple explained that their business policy was whenever they treated a pastor, priest, or minister of the Gospel, it would be free of charge. They had made this decision when they first started their business and had been blessed because of it.

We learned that this couple were born-again Catholics, and the wife had been in one of the meetings where I had spoken not so long ago. She remembered me and had whispered to her husband when I went to pay, "This man is a minister of the Gospel."

It was a total miracle of provision, and we were so elated by God's goodness! I was rejoicing at the Lord's immaculate timing. Had we been able to see the doctor earlier that afternoon, his wife would not have been around as she didn't usually assist her husband, however, she was there that night and remembered me. The fingerprints of God's providence were all over this!

Carol walked out from that clinic with no pain, and her left eye had been saved from blindness. When God works, it is always a perfect work!

We had to return a month later for a check-up, and a month after that, and then another. Up until today, this top eye doctor has been looking after the health of Carol's eyes. Not only did he correct the retinal detachment in her left eye, he also proceeded to fix her right eye, as well as the cataracts in both her eyes. In the last few visits, this doctor has checked my eyes too. Each time we have offered to pay, but never once has he accepted.

I love how God's mathematics work very differently from ours and have learned that I cannot allow my human logic to dictate where and how God will provide. Instead, I must give generously and sacrificially, following the leading of the Holy Spirit.

Carol and I have discovered that we don't need to have a lot, but if we have compassion for those in need, God will provide what is necessary, not just for those in lack, but also for us, who give. We know from experience, that we will *never* be able to outgive God.

CHAPTER TWENTY-THREE

Once life returned to normal after the earthquake, Carol and I resumed our pattern of living between Mount Hope and the bible college. Since the formation of Mount Hope fifteen years earlier, we had divided our time between the two locations, basing ourselves mostly at the bible college but returning to Mount Hope every three months for ten days or so.

We had just returned from a three-monthly visit to Mount Hope, when Ruth, our dean of women, came up to me. "Permissi[8]," she said. "There is a group here to see you both."

We always loved our visits to Mount Hope, but lately I had noticed that the trips took a lot out of me, and it was taking longer to regain my energy after each time. This day I was tired, and was busy preparing my classes for the following week. I really did not have time for unexpected guests, and part of me wanted to stay put.

Ruth is a gracious, wise, and efficient lady who had served us for many years whilst also pastoring a thriving church in Solo. She is more like family than staff, so, putting my work aside, I made my way out to where a group of men were waiting for us. Greeting them cordially, we invited them to sit.

"We are Ahmadiyyah Muslims," said the leader, "but we want to know about Jesus."

Carol's face registered interest. She had just read that the Ahmadiyyah Muslims were being persecuted by other Muslim factions because they were regarded as heretical. The article had said that some had been killed and many were in hiding, fearful for their lives. Now, here was a group of their leaders, sitting in front of us, asking to know more about Jesus.

As Ruth served tea, Carol and I sat and began to share the good news. I

---

[8] Excuse me

noticed some of their faces were expressionless and hard, and they did not seem to be open to my words and yet here they were. It felt like something wasn't quite adding up, but I carried on telling them about Jesus, whilst simultaneously praying for wisdom, knowing that only God can change a heart.

After nearly an hour of talking, they rose to leave, and we made plans to meet again. "We want to bring our friends next time," said the leader of the group. "There are several hundred of us, and you can teach us all about Jesus. There are many that want to know about Him."

At the sound of hundreds of Muslims eager to know Christ, Carol was enthusiastic. After the group left, she immediately turned to me and said, "Wow Sam, this is an amazing opportunity—imagine if they all came to know the Lord!"

I didn't know why, but my excitement levels were not as high as hers. For some reason, there was a question mark in my mind as to the genuineness of this group. Noticing my wariness, Carol assumed that I was afraid of what could happen. Christians who tried to convert Muslims were imprisoned by the government. Alternatively, if the government didn't act, the Muslim community would take matters into their own hands to deal with such situations.

Pushing past my feelings, I picked up the phone and began to call other ministers in our region for their help. If it turned out as the leader had said, hundreds of Ahmadiyyah would need discipling, and I couldn't do this on my own. My hands were full, and we needed others onboard if we were going to be effective in bringing in this potential harvest.

The next few weeks were busy as we made plans to disciple this group. Many responded to the Gospel but were quickly ostracised from their communities. For safety reasons, we couldn't disciple them in their own communities, so we bussed them to various locations for classes. Soon they began asking if they could have longer sessions, and because they were poor, we would house and feed them for two to three days at a time while we brought the Gospel to them. We and our Christian friends and pastors invested much time, finance, and energy into their discipleship and joyfully, many made seemingly genuine decisions and were baptised.

We were yet to find out the truth.

◆ ◆ ◆

"Okay, see you in a couple of days then," I said as I hung up from a call with another pastor. We had just organised yet another baptism service for new believers from the Ahmadiyyah faction. I still had niggling doubts about the conversions but had made the choice to carry on organising the evangelism and discipleship classes. *Even if they weren't completely sincere and had other motives to begin with, maybe as they kept hearing God's Word their attitudes would change?*

Suppressing another yawn, I glanced at my watch and felt my heart drop. I had classes to prepare for tomorrow and my time was fast disappearing—it was going to be another late night to get everything done. Knowing what was on my mind, Carol touched my arm and lightly said "Don't be too late, Sam. You need your sleep."

Her comment irritated me. She was right, of course, but how else was I going to teach the class tomorrow without spending time tonight to get ready? She knew how much I dislike being ill-prepared to speak. I was annoyed, but grudgingly nodded in agreement and kissed her goodnight before making my way back upstairs to my office.

I tried to focus on my teaching material for the next day's class, but my mind kept returning to the upcoming baptism. The location was a four-hour drive away, which didn't thrill me as I was feeling tired, but it couldn't be helped. Indonesia is a big country, and we had chosen a place that was the most central for everyone.

The following day I had a full teaching schedule, and as I walked into my last class I was looking forward to the break at the end. My subject for this class was the gift of healing. This topic was dear to my heart and came not just from my bible knowledge, but also personal experience of seeing God heal people, myself included.

As the lecture was coming to a close, I suddenly felt a surprising weakness come over me, and my left arm felt incredibly heavy. It was a strange sensation, one which was unfamiliar to me. I sat down and asked the students to come and pray, figuring that this was a class on healing, so it seemed like a great opportunity to be healed! They prayed fervently and we all believed for healing, but to our disappointment, nothing happened and the heaviness in my arm did not ease.

Carol knew something was wrong as soon as she saw me walk in the door. "I feel so weak," I explained, "and my left arm just feels so heavy. I'm not sure what I've done to it."

"I think you should go to the doctor, Sam," she said as she rubbed my arm to ease the tightness. Concern was written all over her face.

"No, there's too much to do," I responded, my voice sounding weary. "There's the baptism tomorrow—we can't cancel that. I told them I'd be there."

Carol was looking at me like she wanted to say something else, but she kept quiet. She knew that I didn't like to go back on my word, and once spoken, my word was as good as a promise.

I hopped into bed that night, still feeling weak, and the pervading heaviness in my arm continued to bug me. Sleep came easily, however, and when I woke the next day, my immediate response was to head for the bathroom as usual. I rolled over onto my side to get up, but not only did my left arm still feel heavy, now my left leg wasn't cooperating either. Willing myself to arise, I exerted all my energy, but to no avail—the left side of my body felt like a dead weight, and I literally could not move my leg. This was serious. Worry started to creep into my mind, and I had to fight it by reminding myself that God had not given me a spirit of fear, but of love, power, and a sound mind.

Carol helped me get out of bed, then she quickly packed my things and we drove down to the hospital. I tried to rest in the car while Carol kept things light with conversation and worship music. She was worried, but I could tell she was intentionally putting her trust in the Lord.

The doctor confirmed what we had hoped wasn't true.

I had experienced a stroke that had affected the left side of my body, leaving me with stiffness and weakness. My blood pressure was extremely high, and the doctors immediately worked to relieve some of the pressure. For the next six days I was in the hospital, relearning how to walk and adjusting to the changes in my body. Having lost feeling in my left side, I was unable to move my muscles properly resulting in poor hand-eye coordination, and I had a limp when I walked.

The hospital staff were so encouraging, and my therapist was patient, but I felt frustrated and discouraged by my limited and restricted movements. Although the stroke had not affected my speech or cognitive functions, the diagnosis was such a blow. This was a season of our lives where we needed to be firing on all cylinders. Instead, here I was in the hospital, struggling to open and close my left hand or get my left leg to move again. The physiotherapist had me doing repetitive movements, exercises designed to reignite my muscles to do what should come naturally, but everything was slow, tedious, and hard.

Finally, I was released from the hospital and allowed to go home, which was a relief to me. Upon arriving at the bible college, we were greeted lovingly by the staff who had been praying non-stop for my recovery. The compassionate expressions on their faces moved me, and I was grateful for their love and support. After much hugging and well wishes from the team, I turned and took a few steps towards my house, then abruptly stopped in my tracks outside my front door.

Stairs.

There were three steps up to my house which I had never considered before, but now, suddenly fear overwhelmed me.

I couldn't move any further.

Here I was, Sam Soukotta, the man who had seen God heal many times. I had seen lame people walk again. I knew God could heal and believed He could heal me. But now, I stood there, blocked by a few steps.

Three, to be exact.

I could hardly lift my leg. How was I going to manage this?

The doctor had said I needed to keep moving as much as possible, but when I looked at those three steps, my mind was gripped with fear. What if I tripped and fell?

That's when it dawned on me that there were several large flights of steps on the college campus that I needed to walk up and down many times daily. Last week climbing those steps had been effortless—I didn't even notice them. Now my emotions were running amok just thinking about it.

Turning for help and an arm to lean on, I felt disappointment shroud my shoulders as I slowly shuffled forward. Placing one foot in front of the other, leaning heavily for support, I swung my leg and pulled my body up, one slow step at a time.

The next few weeks were quiet as I wrestled with my new reality.

Carol was so patient with my frustrations and kept encouraging me to do the prescribed exercises. She spent hours rubbing my arm and leg to try and help with the circulation and ease the tension in my shoulders.

My mind kept replaying the last week's incident, and I was annoyed with myself for not heeding my wife's advice to go to the hospital sooner. Perhaps if I had, I would not be in this position now? Frustration set in as I wondered how long it would take for me to completely recover. All my classes and ministry for the rest of the semester were cancelled, and everything felt dark.

What do you want with me, Lord? I questioned one day as I was going through the mundane routine of gripping and releasing my left hand.

As I reflected, snippets of the past year came floating to the surface of my mind, memories of people who had cared enough to warn me about my health. I pictured my doctor's worried face as he prescribed yet another medication for my rising blood pressure. "You need to take it easy for a while," he'd said.

I had suffered from high blood pressure for several years, but lately, the medicines hadn't been as effective. Our lifestyle was at a constant high pace, and we had not taken a holiday in a long time. Travelling for meetings as well as going between Mount Hope and the Bible School had depleted my energy. Although both campuses had great teams running the day-to-day operations, I still held primary responsibility for them, and some days the weight felt almost physical.

The pastors' seminars were an ongoing fixture in our calendar which also required my input, and there were regular visits from pastors, ex-graduates and businesspeople who came for counselling or prayer. Often, they would just turn up at our door without a prior appointment, a normal part of Indonesian culture. On top of all this, I was carrying a considerable amount of the teaching hours on a weekly basis at the bible college.

"You need to rest, Sam," my lovely wife's voice echoed in the chambers of my mind. I had lost count of the times she had said this to me over the last year as she grappled with my bad sleeping patterns. Going to bed late was a habit I had gotten used to, but the last few months had seen me waking early in the morning, often before 4 a.m.

I had been pushing myself; my body had had enough, and it had tried to tell me.

Too foolhardy to slow down or listen to my physical symptoms, my wife, or my doctor, I was now paying the price. Regretting what had happened and my stupidity in creating it, I now had to learn from the experience and carry on.

Slowly, the process of recovery began, but tiredness came quickly as my body readjusted to carrying dead weight. I had to rely more on others to help me take on some of my responsibilities, even with physical things like getting in and out of the car and negotiating all the staircases at the college.

The Lord had placed incredible, caring, competent people all around me, and slowing down allowed me to see them better and learn to rely on them more. God was teaching me humility through this, and I felt like I was a baby Christian again, learning at the feet of my compassionate and loving Father. It was as if my eyes were opened—I became more aware of others who were also suffering physically, and sympathy came more readily now than before.

I was also learning wisdom in how to organise my work-life balance. We still had much to do in life, and God began showing me a pattern for going forward. To be successful in ministry requires maintaining a good balance, and I needed to be more intentional with our rest and holidays. Ministry and calling are not a nine-to-five job. It is all-consuming, and I had allowed it to take over at a cost to my health. Now I had to confront my tendency to drive at an unsustainable pace, relearn the basics of rest and relaxation, and apply a new work pattern.

During this time, I heard that our Muslim discipleship group had fallen apart. Sadly, it had all been a hoax from the start. The leader had used us and many other churches to provide shelter and food for his people as they fled from an opposing faction who wanted to kill them. I couldn't say that this surprised me, as I'd had a niggling feeling about it for a while, but I still felt disappointed by the discovery. My team pointed out that hundreds who wouldn't otherwise have heard the good news now knew of Jesus and owned bibles. There were also several people who made genuine commitments to follow Christ, even though they may have had to keep it secret for their safety.

After four weeks of recuperating, my health had improved enough to take the trip we had booked earlier in the year. We were going to visit our daughter Sheryl and her husband in Washington DC, where she worked for the New Zealand embassy. Both Carol and I were looking forward to being with family again—it was the highlight in our calendar after the last few months.

Two months after the stroke, we travelled to the United States. I was so grateful that the stroke had been mild, and even though I was slow and tired very quickly, I could still walk and talk. Even in America I began to see things that hadn't been so obvious to me previously. People who were suffering seemed to be everywhere—had I just not seen them before? As awareness in me grew, so did sympathy for those who were in physical pain.

◆ ◆ ◆

The stroke and the Ahmadiyyah experience had been difficult experiences for Carol and me as well as our wider team, but we have learned to look for the God-story even in the most disappointing times, knowing the Lord uses these times to develop character. Certainly, this had been a testing time for us. Although relieved to be past the darkest moments, I knew the experience wasn't something to be disregarded.

Scripture tells us that God works all things for good. *All* things! That included my stroke and the Ahmadiyyah hoax. Even though we may not have seen the full extent of God's work amongst that faction, we had done our best and the rest was God's business. On a personal level, experiencing the stroke had taught me lessons I may not have learned otherwise.

Returning to Indonesia two months later, I resumed teaching, although my load was a lot lighter than it had been in the past. For the next year, we cut back on ministry outside the college, and I made relaxation time more of a priority, especially fishing, which was my favourite pastime.

I learned through this, not just to listen, but also to apply the advice of others who God has placed around me, especially those in the medical profession. Although I always respected their recommendations, often I didn't intentionally apply them—or if I did, not for long. My wife Carol is the voice of wisdom in my ear, and I heed her advice readily.

I was grateful that the Lord was teaching me wisdom regarding how to pace myself. I had no idea what was around the corner, but the Lord knew I needed increased capacity and much wisdom to cope with what He wanted us to do next.

CHAPTER TWENTY-FOUR

Scanning through the list of names for the new bible college entrants, I felt the prick of disappointment. The new school year was due to start in a couple of weeks and the number of applications was still incredibly low. The beginning of an academic year had always been an exciting time for our team as we looked forward to meeting all the new students and welcoming back our returning students, but this time it was different. We were just two weeks from starting, and there were only twenty first-year applications. Where were the others?

Along with our four-year degree course at Tawangmangu Bible College, we had also introduced a teacher's training degree. We had earned a reputation in Indonesia for graduating students who were servant-hearted, Kingdom-minded, and had a strong grasp on the Word of God. Many went straight into full-time church service or teaching, and were well-received in churches and schools.

Over the last few years there had been a noticeable downward trend in our student enrolments. When teaching, my classes had felt small compared to the size of the room, and although my students were engaged in the teaching, my mind was often distracted by the empty space. We were a long way from our capacity of one hundred and seventy students.

As I contemplated the situation, I knew something needed to change.

There were several reasons for the drop in student enrolments. Many of the larger churches in the cities were now running their own bible courses. In addition, the financial situation in Indonesia had vastly improved over the last decade, bringing more opportunities for young people, many of whom were choosing to study in bible colleges overseas. These two factors meant fewer students came from the larger cities which affected the financial situation of the college. Our students from the outer islands tended to be poorer, and some still needed to be sponsored. We loved them and would never turn away a student who felt that God was calling them to ministry, just because they couldn't afford to pay the fees. Still, we needed to face the reality of the situation.

What now, Lord? I thought. *What will become of this school?*

My heart felt heavy as I contemplated the situation. This institution had been so blessed by the Lord since its inception in 1968. My in-laws had invested their lives into the vision, and Carol and I had also given many years of our lives. Thousands of graduates were in ministry right across the nation, many of them had planted churches, and the fruit was ongoing.

Nevertheless, without a solution soon we would not be able to continue running the school. Thoughts of doubt and uncertainty for the future of the college were brewing in my mind. Then one day, the Lord reminded me of the beautiful passage in Jeremiah 29:11-13 (NIV):

> *"For I know the plans I have for you," declares the Lord, "plans to prosper you and not to harm you, plans to give you hope and a future. Then you will call on me and come and pray to me, and I will listen to you. You will seek me and find me when you seek me with all your heart."*

This was all the encouragement I needed to go to God and spend time waiting on Him for the way forward.

Carol and I have always seen our journey as a walk of faith. This can sound grand and ethereal, but in fact, living by faith is not the absence of fear or doubt. On many occasions, there has been fear, but when it comes, we draw near to God and spend time with Him. Where possible, I clear my schedule to devote myself to undistracted time with my heavenly Father, whether a few hours, a few days, or a longer season of prayer and fasting and seeking Him in His Word. Even when life is busy and my speaking schedule is full, I try to keep my mind resting on Him and my spirit abiding in Him as I go about my days.

Just as He promised in the passage above, God always speaks to me.

Always.

So that is what I did. Facing uncertainty regarding the future of the bible college, I spent time praying and asking the Lord to show me His way. This time He spoke to me by bringing to mind the story about Elijah in the book of 1 Kings:

> *The Lord said to him, "Go back the way you came, and go to the Desert of Damascus. When you get there, anoint Hazael king over Aram. Also, anoint Jehu son of Nimshi king over Israel, and anoint Elisha son of Shaphat from Abel Meholah to succeed you as prophet."*
>
> 1 Kings 19:15-16

I understood that Hazael and Jehu and Elisha were to carry on the work of Elijah's ministry, but *why did Elijah anoint two kings? I wondered. And what did all this have to do with the bible college? What was God trying to say to me?*

Several months passed, and one day we had a visit from one of our former staff members. She had been a faithful part of our former academic deans and was now a lecturer at a university. A brilliant lady with a servant's heart, we were delighted to see her again and were enjoying catching up, when out of the blue she said, "You should take the next step and turn this college into a university."

Being an academic whose favourite thing in the world is to study and help others in their learning journey, she had mentioned this to me a couple of years earlier, but I hadn't paid any attention. That day, however, her statement caused a light bulb to go off in my head. Carol and I looked at each other and said in tandem, "That's it!"

It was a moment of clarity and revelation for both of us, and we knew in our spirits that this was the way forward for the bible college. God didn't want this college to fizzle out and die—He wanted to take it to a whole new level of expansion!

After our friend left later that afternoon and Carol and I talked it over, it was as if the pieces of a jigsaw puzzle were falling into place, and I felt the Lord bring revelation to the word He had given me several months earlier from the book of 1 Kings.

He showed me that the kings in the passage spoke of marketplace ministry—places where people could have an influential vocation and still have a strong witness for Christ. By becoming a university, we would educate Christian young people to be leaders in their chosen career path and bring God's Kingdom into their workplace. I felt that Elisha represented the continuation of the original bible college as a place where future pastors and church leaders would still be trained. I believed that God was saying to us that the university was going to grow to be twice as big as the theological side—hence the *two* kings.

Upon this realisation, my first thought was, *Where is the money going to come from? This is a huge assignment!*

Then I remembered all God had done for us in the past. He had provided everything for the Mount Hope project and before that, He had provided finance when we needed to build the dormitory at Tawangmangu. The university would certainly be our biggest undertaking yet, but I knew that the Lord had been progressively growing our faith through the other builds, and if this was from the Lord, He would make a way, just like He had before. He would supply not only the money, but also the human resources needed to complete the task.

Having settled this issue, my thoughts jumped to the next problem.

We were based on a mountainside village where there wasn't even a high school, let alone any other tertiary institutions. Tawangmangu was no city, and there were not a lot of highly trained educators nearby. For some, our location may be considered as out of the way. My mind grappled with the question of who would come all this way to help us set up a university?

Several days later I was spending time reading my bible when the story jumped out to me about David and his mighty men. In 2 Samuel 23, David was on the run from the maniacal King Saul who wanted to kill him. David had fled to the remote countryside where he was living in some caves. While in this out-of-the-way place, God brought men to David who became known as his mighty men. These men were acknowledged in their time to be skilful warriors—men who knew how to wield a sword.

Although I wasn't looking to build an army and did not need warriors, I knew we were going to need skilled and professional people to form a university. Our core team of staff at the bible college were fantastic, faithful, and hardworking, but we were going to need different skills, high level training, and expertise for something that none of my team—myself included—knew much about.

Neither Carol nor I had studied at university. Carol had left school a year early to support herself, and after high school, I had gone straight to bible college for three years and gained a diploma in ministry. Neither of us had any idea how to start a university.

Reading the story of David, I felt the Lord was encouraging me. I knew my heavenly Father would not ask me to do something without providing the resource, which in this case was the right people.

Just as He brought the mighty men to help David win his battles, I believed God was going to bring the right professionals along to help us with the formation of this educational institution. All we needed to do was find out who they were and ask them for help.

As Carol and I prayed and talked it over, we suddenly remembered Inge, the woman who we had met and worked with, along with her husband, almost ten years ago during the Bantul earthquake rebuild project. Inge was now a lecturer in several universities in Java, and although we weren't sure she had experience with founding a university, I figured she would know a lot more than we did.

I picked up my cell phone and dialled her number, which she promptly answered. As it happened, she had just spent a day convening with a group of people from the Department of Education. The topic of conversation for the day was, "How to start new government-approved universities in Java."

God was all over this, I could feel it! This group had formed to bring consistency to tertiary education in the country. Up until this point, any organisation could set up a 'university' without adhering to the nationally endorsed curriculum, and students were graduating with sub-standard degrees. The government was now working to close these schools and were looking to get behind institutions that would teach the nationally endorsed curriculum.

I quickly described our vision to Inge over the phone and she excitedly said, "I'll put Tawangmangu university on the list!" From that day, although I hadn't asked her, she started working on the government permit for us.

God's mighty men are also God's mighty women!

◆ ◆ ◆

The permit to start a university was not easy to come by, nor was it cheap. We needed about eight thousand dollars—a large amount of money, which we didn't currently have. There was a small amount in the college savings account but not enough, so we started by investing our income for that month.

We have found that whenever God has asked Carol and I to begin a new venture, it has been initiated by what we have in our own hands—or, to be more specific, in our bank account. This is a principle of faith that we have learned and live by—start by giving what we have. Carol and I can personally testify that we have never had to strive to outwork a vision, as God has provided for our personal needs every time.

Once we had given our money, we then challenged our staff and students to also give what they could. At our following Sunday morning service, we took up an offering for the permit, and prayed over the giving. When the offering money was counted we were astounded at the amount that had come in. In that service there happened to be a visitor from Solo who had come to attend the meeting. He was not a regular, and had no prior knowledge of the offering we were going to receive, but he was moved to give. The generous giving of this visitor, on top of what our college residents put in, came to the largest amount we had ever received from within the college.

We were extremely encouraged. Joyfully, we now had enough to pay for the permit, which we submitted immediately.

A few weeks later, Inge rang us to say that the Education Department had received over thirty applications from different entities wanting to build new universities in central Java. Of those thirty, only two permits were granted—one of which was ours!

We were jubilant! We lived in a Muslim nation, and had been upfront about the fact that our university was going to be a Christian university. Gaining approval seemed unlikely from the start, but when God gives the go-ahead, He also clears the way.

In June 2018, fifty years since my in-laws had started the Tawangmangu Bible College, we laid the first foundation stone for the new university building. I felt humbled and moved by the greatness of God in getting us to this point. It was a poignant moment as we broke ground and laid the first stone signifying the ongoing plan that the Lord had for the college.

CHAPTER TWENTY-FIVE

Three months later, a Chinese businessman and his wife were holidaying in Tawangmangu when they happened to bump into a mutual acquaintance of ours. When they asked what brought her to the area, she mentioned she had come to see us and invited them to meet us too. They took her up on the offer as they had no agenda for the day and were intrigued to see the college campus.

Our friend introduced us and as we spent time chatting and getting to know them, we discovered they were elders in their local church in Solo. They were extremely interested in the bible college and asked plenty of questions about its history, the students, and how it was run. We talked in length about the exciting changes that were about to happen on our campus with the development of a new university. After coffee and good conversation, they thanked us and said their goodbyes, and we all parted company.

Not long after their visit, this couple discovered that the husband had pancreatic cancer and was already in the advanced stages. It shocked them both to the core. Filled with grief and concern about the future for his wife and business, he became gripped by fear. This affected him so much that he went off food, stopped showering, and was unable to cope with the day-to-day business of life.

His wife tried everything to encourage her husband to keep hoping in God, but her efforts were futile. Not knowing what to do, she gave us a call to ask if we would come and pray for him. She said that when they were talking to us at the college, they had felt their faith rise, and it had impacted them so much they had talked about it for the whole hours' drive home. She wanted this faith for her husband who had lost his hope and needed help.

We happened to be returning from some meetings in Jakarta, and after landing in Solo we decided to visit their home to encourage and pray for him before heading back to Tawangmangu.

After our visit the man's wife reported to us that he noticeably improved, so over the following weeks I called him regularly to encourage him and try to build his faith through prayer and the Word of God. The sick businessman appreciated my time, and we could see that his faith was strengthened through my phone calls and the occasional visit.

Two months later we were holding meetings in the city of Bandung when we received a phone call from the same man. He told us he was about to send a substantial sum of money for the construction of the university. It was an astounding amount, the largest sum we had ever received, enough that he had to send it in three different transactions to avoid suspicion of money laundering from the Indonesian government! We were beyond excited! We had already commenced building the new university with small amounts that had come through, but this donation was going to give it a very good push! All going to plan, we were on track to complete stage one.

◆ ◆ ◆

By the following year the man's cancer was in advanced stages, and he was hospitalised in Singapore. Until now we had been regularly visiting him in Solo to encourage him and pray for his healing, and he always seemed to respond so well to our visits. His wife told us that he would brighten up and gain a bit of strength—as if he was leaning on us for his faith.

Good friends of ours encouraged us to visit him in Singapore, and booked the flights for us to spend some time with him, not knowing that this would be the last time we saw him. Soon after our trip, the Lord took him to heaven, where we know he is now completely healed.

Unbeknown to us, just before he passed away, he told a friend by the name of Pak Hardede that he must meet us. So it was, that one day, out of the blue, Pak Hardede turned up at our house and introduced himself. We got to know him and had a nice conversation, reminiscing about our mutual friend who had recently died. After his visit we carried on with our day, and thought no more about him.

◆ ◆ ◆

By the middle of 2019 the first stage of the construction on the university building was complete. This gave us underground parking, spacious first-floor classrooms, and several bathrooms. Our friend's donation had allowed us to build a roof, but at this point the second and third storeys were only a shell, with no walls, windows, or internal rooms.

Having now run out of funds, the work had come to a halt. I knew we would need a significant amount to finish the project, but we had used all our resources, and no more donations had come in for the last few months.

We cried out to God and waited for His provision.

One month passed, then two months, then three, and still nothing.

As we carried on doing what we had in front of us and were faithful with teaching the students who were going through college, we kept trusting in the Lord to provide.

Seven months later there was still no movement on the building site. By this point, we (and the rest of the world) had our eyes on China as the Covid-19 pandemic erupted.

Over the next few months we watched as the pandemic gripped the nations and changed the way our world lives, forever. Thousands in our nation died, many simply because they did not have access to oxygen tanks.

The Indonesian government did everything they could to encourage the public to take the necessary precautions to stay healthy, but it was a sad time for many. In such a hugely populated country where many live in very close proximity to each other, the virus spread swiftly and the hospitals were unable to cope with the burden of the sick. We were saddened to hear that people were dying at home, unable to get the medical treatment they needed.

At the college, we implemented strict safety protocols to keep everyone safe, and limited all movement to the outside community. We had sanitizing misters installed at our entrance gates to spray disinfectant solution on all who entered. Several rooms were designated as isolation rooms for those who had a sore throat or a cough. Precautions such as wearing masks and washing hands were a way of life for us now, although social distancing was sometimes tricky when everyone lived on the same campus.

Although we heard of a few deaths in the local community of Tawangmangu, we felt so blessed that there weren't many, and especially that we were able to keep the virus at bay within our campus walls. As much as possible, we carried on with classes and our daily routines throughout this time.

By now, almost a year and a half had passed since the building project had stalled and I began to wonder if I had made a mistake. *Had I heard God correctly about starting a university?* I could see the half-built university from my bedroom, and each time I looked out my window, it was a reminder of a promise yet unfulfilled. The start of the new school year was looming, and we had hoped to open the university in September, but everything looked stacked against us.

I felt so sure that the Lord had directed us to this point. He had provided incredibly to get us this far. We believed the university was His idea, yet here we were with an unfinished building, no money in our account to complete it, no donations for months, and to top it all off, a global pandemic which slowed everything down further!

Where are you, Lord? I wondered. *What are we to do now?*

Inge was still working tirelessly on our case, and despite the ups and downs of the pandemic, she had managed to acquire the phone number of a leading figure in the Department of Education in Indonesia. Inge had rung the lady and spoken to her about the vision behind the university. The government official was so taken by our venture that she took it upon herself to promote our project, and it had gained the attention of the higher authorities. To our surprise, one day in the middle of the year, we received a phone call from the Department of Education. The person on the other end of the call told us that the government wanted to back us, and were offering to sponsor the first intake of students by paying their fees for their whole four-year degree!

We could not believe what we were hearing. Our Indonesian government—a *Muslim* government—was telling us they would pay for all the initial students who came to study at our *Christian* university, not just for their first year but for all four years of their tuition! This was amazing favour! I felt so buoyed by this and knew the Lord was encouraging us to go ahead with the opening despite the unfinished building.

Our team set about planning, and with careful logistics we knew we would be able to run the university and bible college simultaneously, even with partial use of the new building. We already had the first floor completed, and this was a good usable space for classrooms, plus we could use the bible college dormitories for living spaces for both the university and college students.

God was showing us that *He* would make a way, even in a worldwide pandemic. Sure enough, as the proposed opening neared, we were excited to see applications come in. By the time September came around, we had sixty students enrolled into one of our three departments. We had decided to begin by offering degrees in hospitality and tourism, business and management, and visual communication design.

Kicking off the new school year with an uncompleted building was not what I had envisioned and yet, here we were with sixty university students and eighty bible college students happily attending their classes! Even though the pressure for the building project was still there, I delighted in the way that God's work carries on despite chaos and imperfection.

◆ ◆ ◆

In October 2020, over a year after we had first met, Pak Hardede came to pay us another visit. We were happy to see him again and were enjoying small chit-chat when he blurted out that he too wanted to help us with the building project. Surprised by his comment, we asked him what he meant by 'helping'.

He told us that he was a developer and owned his own building company, and that if we were keen, he was prepared to go ahead with the building project and we could just pay him as the funds came in, even if he had to financially back the project for a while. We communicated clearly to him that the building had stalled for almost eighteen months because there was no ongoing support. We were doing the best we could with what we had by trying to stretch the bible college income to save up for the building, but we still had students who were slow in paying their fees. Pak Hardede understood the situation and repeatedly assured us that he would rather put his own money into the building than see the project stalled.

This was *not* how I had imagined our prayers being answered! I had half expected the Lord to bring along a sponsor, whether a person or a church, as He had done in the past, to cover our needs. Yet, we had seen God move in unusual ways before and understood that He didn't work according to our expectations or formulas. Just because it didn't look like the provision I was expecting, didn't mean that it wasn't God's way for us at this moment. I had to get comfortable with the way that He was providing a solution for us now.

As we watched the building progress, my burden slowly began to lift. Pak Hardede was brilliant at his job and his workmen were quick but thorough.

By the end of February 2021, the construction was complete. In four months, Pak Hardede had been able to finish the three-storey building, which now included extra classrooms, teachers' spaces, a technology suite, and offices, along with the underground parking. It was a beautiful building, and as Carol and I stood at the dedication, I was moved by how God had brought this about, starting with our sick friend who was now with the Lord. It had been such a long process but here we were rejoicing as we stood in front of another testimony to God's amazing faithfulness.

We now had two tertiary institutions operating simultaneously, and our administration and teaching team had to adjust our building and space usage to accommodate the scheduling of both the university and the bible college. Our main hall was too small to accommodate both schools at the same time, so we ran the schools separately even though the students all lived on the same campus.

We noticed from the start that many of the university students came from nominal faith backgrounds, and although they thought of themselves as Christians, many had not experienced a personal relationship with Jesus. However, as they got to know the bible college students who were passionate about their relationships with Christ, change began happening in many of the university students. We saw a hunger for God began to stir in them which became increasingly apparent as many became more invested in the worship services and prayer gatherings.

At the conclusion of my sermon one Sunday I decided to give a salvation invitation—something I rarely did in our bible college services, as I was already preaching to the converted, so to speak. This time, however, many of the university students responded by giving their hearts to Jesus, and before the year was up, they had all either made a new commitment to follow Christ or freshly dedicated their lives to Him. My team and I had not expected this when we were caught up in the busyness of the building stages, nor was this something we had foreseen in all those months of waiting for provision. But God knew. His hand of providence had brought these young people to us, not only for training for a future career, but also for their salvation.

Clearly, the Lord's hand had been on this project from the start. We had seen miracle after miracle, and more were unfolding in front of us now. This was encouraging to us—and proof that when things in the world are topsy-turvy, as they so often are, it's still business as usual in the Kingdom of God.

By May 2021, as the first year of the university came to a close, we already had enrolments and a wait list for the next intake. Today we are once again at capacity, which is fantastic. In fact, due to space constraints we have had to cap the intake for both the university and the bible college while we look for more land to build another dormitory.

Building the university was a journey of faith for Carol and me. When I first started talking to the Lord in 2015 about our declining student roll, I could not have imagined that five years later we would have a university running alongside the bible college. This project stretched us financially, intellectually, and spiritually. That God would ask two people with no university education to build one is proof that He uses the foolish things of the world to confound the wise. We were way beyond our comfort zone as we gathered to talk about curriculum, governance, and education but the Lord brought the right people around us each step of the way. In our eyes, they were the mighty men and women God had added to our team.

CHAPTER TWENTY-SIX

Over the years, one of the most rewarding aspects of our ministry has been seeing how God is using many of the graduates from our schools, bible college, and university. We now have alumni serving in Kyrgyzstan, the United States, New Zealand, Australia, Holland, parts of South-East Asia, and of course, hundreds all over Indonesia. Some are businesspeople, others are teachers, and many are pastors, all serving their communities, whether in large cities, small villages, or the remote islands. Each one has incredible stories of what God is doing through them. We wouldn't be able to write them all, but I want to leave you with the story of Titus and Artha...

◆ ◆ ◆

The man's shabby clothes were torn and dirty. His hair was dishevelled, his eyes blank as he aimlessly wandered down the street muttering to no one, a cackle of laughter randomly erupting from his lips.

As Titus watched him, the man stopped at a rubbish bin and began to rummage through it, seemingly oblivious to the rank odour and swarming flies as he picked out various morsels to eat. Compassion began to well up in Titus' heart as he wondered who this man was. Clearly, he was homeless and mentally challenged, and judging by what he was having for breakfast, unable to look after himself properly.

Unable to stand by and watch any longer, Titus approached the man and began to talk to him, asking if he would like to come to his house for a proper meal and a place to stay.

Titus' own home was far from comfortable. On graduating from Tawangmangu Bible College, he and his wife, Artha, had spent some time pastoring in a large city church but had recently laid that down and moved to Solo. Although they knew God had called them to this new city, they were unsure what they were supposed to do. Times were tough and they were renting a small house—its only positive feature being that it was cheap. *My house is still better than no house*, Titus reasoned as he and his passenger motored home.

A couple of weeks later, as I walked into their simple house to visit, I saw Titus sitting on the floor, playing the guitar and worshipping the Lord. A man was sitting next to him whom I hadn't met, but I guessed he was the homeless man Titus had found. The man was calm, clean, and dressed in nice clothes. He was also singing along with Titus.

On our next visit, a month or so later, walking into their living room, we saw Titus sitting in the same place on the floor playing his guitar, but now there wasn't just one man beside him. The first man had been joined by a few more men who sat on the floor, cross-legged, as he played. All were mentally handicapped, and up until recently, all were homeless. They had been left by their families to drift on the streets and rummage through rubbish bins for whatever food they could find.

There are many people like this in Indonesia, and the government does not have enough capacity to house and look after them. With no social system to care for the homeless, it is left to the goodness of locals to give them food or money. Often, because of their behavioural tendencies, which at times are erratic, people are afraid of interacting with them, and leave them alone to fend for themselves.

As Titus and Artha took these people in and looked after them, they realised this was their new mission. Morning and night they would gather their new family together to teach them songs about God and worship with them. They prayed daily for them and loved on these people who society had seemingly forgotten. Some of them were so far gone in their minds that they couldn't control their bodily functions and would make much mess around the house, which Artha and Titus had to clean up. Patiently they taught these people basic hygiene and how to look after themselves. Not unlike teaching children, daily repetition and much patience was needed.

Over time and as they built trust in the community, others came alongside to help Titus and Artha. A local doctor gave his time to make regular checks on the patients and was amazed to see how their mental health was improving through the simple investment of time, love, and care in an atmosphere of praise and worship.

Years have passed since Titus and Artha took the first man in. Today they have a beautiful building with dormitories for men and women—a place where they regularly care for one hundred and eighty patients, some who reside long term, and others who come for a short while.

Sinae, the name of their organisation, has built a reputation throughout Indonesia for taking in mentally-challenged people and seeing many of them restored to health without the use of any medication.

In the mid-2000's, the local council approached Titus and Artha to ask if they could start looking after drug addicts. This was a growing concern in the city, and the government did not have the resources to address the situation. They had seen Titus and Artha's fantastic track record with difficult situations over the years and were very keen to work with them. It was a win-win arrangement, as the government scheme also enabled a steady income for Sinae.

A few years later the head of the Social Welfare department of Indonesia personally invited Artha to accompany her on a trip to several Asian countries to learn how other governments handle drug problems. This couple's commitment, sacrifice, and faithfulness to the task God had given them was opening doors to impact a nation at the highest level. Their story also motivated other churches and mission workers to start similar homes in other parts of Indonesia.

Titus and Artha, a humble couple who had absolutely no training with the mentally disabled, the homeless, or drug addicts, have been so used by God to help vulnerable people and their families, and are now being sought after by the Indonesian government as partners.

Carol and I watch on with amazement as we see what God is doing with Titus and Artha—and with the hundreds of other ex-students who we have had the privilege of discipling and walking with.

We know the story has just begun.

AFTERWORD

Starting a university, building two hundred simple houses for earthquake victims, taking in three siblings from the jungle, rescuing a hundred and forty orphans, discipling thousands of students to follow Jesus, or founding Mount Hope . . . none of these were our ideas, or even things we would have imagined doing. We were simply willing to listen.

Regardless of how God speaks, whether through the bible, other people, or by speaking to us directly, my wife and I have learned over the years that He will provide what is needed for the next step, whether it is money, strength, wisdom, protection or people.

Whenever we have taken the first step in response to what the Lord has said, our faith becomes alive. It stretches, it grows—it's living!

Living faith causes you to act on what you believe.

In my experience, God is speaking all the time, and throughout our journey, Carol and I have always endeavoured to listen and act.

Listen and act.

Listen and act.

By simply partnering with God, we have seen amazing things unfold. None of this would have been possible in our own abilities or strength.

I will never regret the decision the seventeen-year-old me made all those years back when I chose, despite rejection from my family, to follow Jesus. The day that I walked out of my grandparents' home and turned my back on my uncle's fury is forever etched in my mind, but God had seen my obedience. Years later, when Carol and I went back to visit my family, it was a much different scenario as my uncle, softened by the years, pulled Carol and me in and hugged us, tears rolling down his face as he asked for forgiveness.

We have learned over many decades to walk confidently in faith, trusting that our heavenly Father truly does have the best in mind for us. He will always make a way, even when we can't see a path with our physical eyes.

Now, as we survey the bible college and university grounds, we are once again feeling the pinch of space and are needing to stretch again to find more land to build on. Although we are both now in our seventies, we have learned in this journey of faith that you never actually arrive—until you get to heaven, that is! We may never understand why there have been seasons of waiting, sorrow, questioning, threats and even persecution, but we have learned that we are not promised an effortless journey when we follow the Lord. The rewards, however, absolutely outweigh the cost. What I do know, is that when we walk and work with the God of the universe, anything can happen!

Carol and I have given our lives to following our Saviour's call, and we will continue to do so until the end. There is no greater experience and no greater cause.

World Outreach team ministering in Death Row,
Muntinlupa Prison

World Outreach Literature Centre Team,
Philippines 1968

Asaph Team, Indonesia

Sam and Carol's Wedding

Sam and the crowd at an early crusade

Carried to the meeting. Now walking freely

Crowds of all ages

No more crutches!

Healed after 12 years of paralysis

The Soukotta Family.
Sheryl, Sam, Ronn, Jeffrey, Carol, Marissa

Bible College students singing

Sam teaching a class of Bible College students

Mount Hope Primary School kids in a class activity.
Dorms and classrooms in the background

Mount Hope school kids with the Mount Hope Hill in the background

Our first intake of university students

The now complete university building

Sam and Carol

ACKNOWLEDGEMENTS

Sam and Carol would like to thank:

The Assemblies of God NZ and World Outreach who have supported us since the start of our journey both financially and in prayer.

Our team of staff at the Tawangmangu Bible College who are so loyal and have stood beside us and worked with us for many years. Special mention goes to Yehezkiel and Ernik Tunliu and Ruth Suphia who have been with us since the very early days. We thank the Lord for you.

Abraham and Melani Siregar and the amazing team at Mount Hope. We appreciate you and value your servant hearts. Thank you for your ongoing work.

Craig Pilcher, who helped with much of the building at Mount Hope, and to Francee for sharing Craig with us, sometimes for weeks on end.

Rob and Fiona Reid, for your ongoing love and encouragement of us and our family. We are very grateful.

Petrus and Inge Widodo, who have been so instrumental in setting up and registering the university in Tawangmangu.

The countless many who we have come across at some point in our journey. We are so grateful to the Lord for you.

Marissa would like to thank:

My heavenly Father for speaking to me from the start and for making a way for this book to happen. I am humbled and awed by Your providence. Thank you for calling me to partner with You.

My wonderful husband Richard, for encouraging me every step of the way in this project. Thank you for picking up the slack on the days when I was juggling too many things and for keeping me steady. This book would not have happened without you. *Saya cinta kamu.*

Elijah, Ethan and Arielle, I don't think there are three better kids anywhere! Thank you for being patient and for cheering me on. I love you so much.

Mum and Dad for embarking on this venture with me and for your support and faith in me. May many be inspired by your story.

Mike and Jeannie, the best in-laws a girl could have! Thank you so much for your many words of encouragement, ongoing prayer support and love.

Sheryl, my lovely sister and Michael for the help with the sketch and my photos. Ronn and Rochelle for the thoughtful advice and Jeff and Eva for creating the website. Also special mention to Eden, Leah and Layla-Grace (and baby Sammy). Thank you all for the many laughs and for being my family.

Anya McKee and the team at Torn Curtain Publishing. Thank you for walking me through this and the hours you have poured into it. This book is almost as much a labour of your love as mine. Your reassurance and professionalism are just what I needed with this project. Thank you, my friends.

Josh and Jo Barr for jumping in on the vision right at the start with your photography skills.

Mikey Mann for the cover design. It's perfect, *terima kasih banyak!*

Maggie, you've been a pastor and personal cheer leader to me. Thank you for the prophetic words and the consistent intercession. I am grateful for you.

My pastors, Boyd and Sharon Ratnaraja and the staff team at Elim Wellington. Thank you for being so understanding and for releasing me from other ministry commitments to focus on writing this book. I am ever grateful to you.

My church family and many friends, I thank you for caring enough to ask 'how it's going', and for your warm encouragement and prayers for me as I wrote this book. Here it is at last! I hope you are blessed by it.

To learn more about the Soukottas and their ongoing story, visit:
www.soukotta.com

www.ingramcontent.com/pod-product-compliance
Lightning Source LLC
Chambersburg PA
CBHW032337300426
44109CB00041B/1120